Maja and Me

My Journey with My Lesbian Daughter

Mary Rose Knutson

Paddle Press

The author is available to speak to book groups, PFLAG
chapters, church groups, and any other interested audiences.
You may contact her at knutsonmary@gmail.com.

To Maja,

who has had many supporting roles in her life and now deserves to be

THE SHINING STAR!

Contents

Prelude

I will go, Lord, if you lead me.

—"Here I Am, Lord"

I enter the church quietly. No one else is there. I walk down the center aisle and slide into a long wooden pew near the front. I gaze up at the wooden ceiling beams, which remind me of the hull of a ship. The grandeur of the pointed arches above them creates a feeling of insignificance for one person in such a large sanctuary. The stone walls accentuate the firmness of a foundation. Truly it is an omnipotent place, bringing forth a belief that God is in this cathedral, ready to hear my prayers and guide me forward. I look up at the marble altar with the white cross and focus on light shining through the stained-glass picture of Jesus ascending into heaven. It reminds me of his love for everyone, which makes Jesus the perfect example. I feel ready to listen and follow where he will lead me.

I bow my head in silent prayer, and the words of a hymn float into my mind.

> Here I am, Lord. Is it I, Lord?
> I have heard you calling in the night.
> I will go, Lord, if you lead me.
> I will hold your people in my heart.

I feel an invisible tap on my shoulder. God has heard the people crying, and I wonder, *Who are these people? Could they possibly be gays and lesbians asking for God's help? Could it possibly be my daughter asking for God's help? What message is about to be revealed to me?*

Could God be calling me to help take the message to those who have been persecuting gays and lesbians? Could God be calling me to help take the message to those who are persecuting my daughter? Could God's love break through in each of these people and help them respond with a change of heart, letting their love for others shine through?

I feel warmth, rays of light giving me a gentle massage, and the words "Is it I, Lord?" keep ringing in my ears.

Here I am Lord, is it I Lord?

Are you sure you want me? God keeps tapping and calling until I respond.

I will go, Lord, if you lead me.
I will hold your people in my heart.

I believe God is the source of this gentle, persistent drip of water that will eventually make a hole through the stone. God keeps giving me taps and nudges until finally the pathway becomes clear.

So here I am, Lord, writing a book to tell the story of Maja and me in hopes that it will help more people to listen with their hearts, learn with their minds, and accept LGBTQ* people and include them with their whole being.

---

*"LGBTQ" stands for lesbian, gay, bisexual, transgender, and queer or questioning. While I often say "gays and lesbians" in everyday conversation, in this book I'm choosing to use more inclusive language, as I've grown to understand more about the community my daughter is part of.

Prologue

My mom and dad were born in Denmark. They taught me Danish ways, and I spoke Danish before I learned English. One of the concepts I learned was *hyggelig* (pronounced "hue-guh-lee" with hard *g*s), a word that encompasses the English words *warm, safe, secure, pleasant, cozy, comforting,* and *restful,* all rolled into one.

Hyggelig describes our living room perfectly. At every time of year it is a hyggelig place to be. My favorite spot is the wooden chair upholstered in blue velvet that sits by the front window, next to the radiator. The chair creaks whenever I settle into it. The padded back, seat, and arms give me a sense of hyggelig calmness. The chair comforts me, as does a mug of steaming spice tea. Our house is one hundred plus years old, and we have lived here for over forty of those. Its built-in stained bookcases and ceiling beams provide comfort and radiate a message of welcome.

When the sun streams in through the large, double-hung windows, it casts shadows across the furniture, and I see the dust on the wood floors, wooden chairs, and woodwork. Though I'm the house cleaning lady, I have a "Who cares?" attitude as I curl up on the love seat for a nap or to read a book, enjoying the sun warming my body.

I frequently look up from my reading to take a sip of tea and just enjoy my time here. The many framed, cross-stitched embroideries I have made hang on the walls. The watercolor masterpiece of irises that a friend painted holds the place of honor over the mantel.

The blue-and-white Danish Christmas plates on the plate rack in the adjoining dining room soothe me, as do our antique table, the windows on one side, and the built-in buffet. Looking at them, I feel content.

This hyggelig feeling also energizes me when I remember conversations in this room with our family and friends. I can picture Maja sitting on the love seat at the age of three, anxious to go out trick-or-treating for the first time, waiting for her big sister, Siri, who had just celebrated her sixth birthday.

Maja was a fireman that year. She had on her red raincoat, and I made her a fireman's hat out of red construction paper. I was adjusting Siri's wig. Siri had red hair as a baby, so she'd always been attracted to Raggedy Ann, and that's who she was for Halloween.

As I take another sip of tea I smile, remembering Maja's exuberance when she came back from trick-or-treating that evening. She was excited about the candy, but also about being outside after dark and ringing all the neighbors' doorbells. For weeks afterward, she would tell people all about it.

About a month or so later, Maja and I were sitting on the love seat reading a book together. The book was titled *What Will I Be When I Grow Up?* I had noticed that when people asked Maja what she wanted to be when she grew up, she would say without the slightest hesitation, "A fireman." I got to thinking about her response. Did she actually know the job of a fireman? Perhaps I had told her that firemen have important work: they save people in distress; they come to their rescue when a fire is about to destroy their home. So I asked her, "What do firemen do?" She replied, "They go from door to door and get candy."

It was in this most loving place, eighteen years later, that Maja and I started a conversation that would point us both in a new direction.

1

Mom, I Have Something to Tell You

Behold, I am doing a new thing: now it springs forth, do you
not perceive it?

—Isaiah 43:19a ESV

It was the first year of a new century. Maja was about to begin her
senior year of college at Augustana College in Sioux Falls, South
Dakota. One summer evening, after one of those special days—not too
hot, not too humid—the windows were open in the living room, and a
gentle breeze blew in, cooling our bodies as we sat together on the love
seat. Maja's blonde hair had grown long again. It was pulled back with
a binder. Her shorts and T-shirt revealed her physically fit body; she
spent her summers working at camps, carrying canoes, and swimming.
My gray hair, now turning to silver, hadn't necessarily contributed to
my wisdom, but I too felt most comfortable wearing Bermuda shorts
and a T-shirt. I liked wearing Maja's cast-off Ts. They made me feel
closer to her. Maja and I both have short legs, so the love seat fits our
bodies perfectly. It lets us sit close together for intimate talks.

I sometimes pondered what Maja's character was really all about.
She could be comical, creative, and witty. Sometimes she would sit and
be perfectly still. Her deep-set eyes seemed to be concentrating inward.
What memories and deep thoughts did she have that she didn't readily
share? To strive to be two adults sharing thoughts and ideas—to build
a sense of trust and love—was what we both wanted. Or was that just

what I envisioned? Sometimes I felt we were close, and other times I felt a wall go up between us.

"Mom, I have something to tell you." I could see by the way Maja had set her jaw and pressed her lips together that this was going to be a serious conversation. She swallowed hard and waited for my response. What was she going to tell me? Was she pregnant? Dropping out of college? The tone of her voice triggered a warning bell. My stomach became queasy; my muscles tensed up. I just nodded for her to continue.

Her shoulders rose as she took several deep breaths, looked at me, and then looked away. Struggling to get the words out, looking down at her hands clasped tightly together, she looked at me again.

"Mom, I think I'm gay."

Maja watched my face, searching for my reaction. Did my mouth curl downward in an expression of disgust? Were my eyes revealing my rejection? I'm not sure she could interpret my thoughts.

I wasn't fully getting the message. I wanted to say something, but nothing registered.

This safe place on the love seat had suddenly turned into a canoe in rough seas. Our family valued time spent paddling in our canoe, which was wide and not tippy. It had always seemed like a safe place. But now no one was in control. Cold water hit my face, and instinctively I shut my eyes tight and quit breathing altogether.

After a long pause, I looked at Maja and said, "I thought you were going to tell me you were pregnant." She had just broken up with her boyfriend. We both laughed—stilted laughter, uncomfortable laughter. My arm instinctively went around Maja's shoulders.

We sat there for a while in silence. Maja looked at me with her hazel eyes and determined, serious face. Outwardly I must have appeared calm, but within I felt frozen. My only thought was, *My little sweet girl thinks she's gay? Does she know for sure? Is there a slight hope that she isn't?* I took my arm down from around her shoulders.

Setting my knee further onto the love seat, I finally turned to look directly into my daughter's eyes and said, "You know, when you were a little girl and bumped your head, I could automatically feel that hurt. My head would jerk back as if I had bumped my head too. But now I can only empathize. Sadly, this time I can't go to that same place with you."

Maja continued looking at me. Was she expecting me to say more to comfort her? Was she looking for my acceptance, or did she think I would be angry and reject her?

We remained on the love seat for some time, not talking, just being together. I noticed the light in the room was growing dim; shadows loomed up in a foreboding manner. Clouds covered the sun as it faded and set over the horizon. I broke the silence.

"I love you, Maja, no matter what."

2

I'll Love You More Than Anybody Can

The Lord is near to the brokenhearted and saves the crushed in spirit.

—Psalm 34:18

We both slowly got up from the love seat, and I enfolded Maja in my arms. My eyes filled with tears. The thought *Maja thinks she's gay* was still ringing in my ears. I tried to remain calm, although my heart was racing and I couldn't seem to come up with words of encouragement for Maja. Instead, I gave her another loving hug and hoped she would understand my unexpressed feelings through our physical closeness.

There was a slight smile on Maja's face. I tried to respond to her smile with a more pleasant smile of my own, but my slumped shoulders, bearing a heavy burden of sadness, prevented me from giving Maja the love I felt deep inside.

I realized I had been invited in.

Maja is coming out, and I am coming in.

I had absolutely no idea what all this would mean other than feeling completely frozen with fear.

I wish I had taken Maja, sat her on my lap in the old blue velvet chair, put my arms around her, and held her tight. I could have sung to her just like when she was a little girl; I could have hummed one of her favorite songs, and soon we would both have felt better. But this time I wanted Maja to soothe me.

4

Together we walked up the stairs, each in our own world. I watched her close the door to her bedroom. In our family, closed doors meant *Don't disturb me now*. If the door was closed, it was usually not a good sign.

I went through the motions of getting ready for bed. Paul wasn't home. He was away at a science conference, giving a lecture. We could not grieve together. I couldn't phone and tell him either. Maja had said she wanted to tell her dad herself, so I had to keep this inside until a time when she could tell him in person.

Keep it inside and not tell him? How am I going to do that?

I wished Maja had waited and told both of us together. But I had promised her I wouldn't say anything, and I wanted her to know she could trust me. I left it up to her as to when she wanted to come out to Dad.

Our antique four-poster bed didn't provide the usual comfort. The warmth of the summer evening prevented me from snuggling into the covers. Falling asleep didn't seem possible. An overwhelming sense of loss engulfed me. Frustration, mourning, and sadness were setting in. I wanted to be strong for Maja, but I wanted to ask so many questions. This would be a whole new way of life for her and for us, too.

I lay in bed with eyes wide open in the middle of the night. I kept looking at the clock, thinking about Maja. As the minutes ticked by, my mind seemed stuck. I couldn't even think of the future and where that might lead us. My thoughts just kept spinning. Perhaps it was my prayers, talking to God, asking for guidance that finally gave me a sense of calmness and peace. These words came into my mind:

> Be still and know that I am God.
> Be still and know that I am with you.
> Be still and know that I will comfort you
> When you come to Me in your hour of need.
> I will wipe away your tears . . .
> I am present in your pain.

I will give you rest.

I will give you peace.

I kept thinking of people rejecting Maja; I was fearful that harm could come to her. Sadness seeped through my thoughts. Would she have struggles about her identity that could leave her less confident in what she might aspire to become?

I have never been a mom who expressed her inner feelings to her children. I always figured they knew that by my actions. I realized I needed to tell them more often how much I loved them.

Finally, since sleep was not possible, I sat up in bed and began to read a book on my nightstand. The words on the page floated into my brain but got jumbled up inside. I didn't comprehend anything I read. My mind kept repeating the phrase *I'll love you more than anybody can. I'll love you more than anybody can* . . .

Be still . . .

3

Special Delivery

And a woman who held a babe against her bosom said, Speak
   to us of Children.
And he said:
Your children are not your children.
They are the sons and daughters of Life's longing for itself.
They come through you but not from you,
And though they are with you yet they belong not to you.

                     —Kahlil Gibran, *The Prophet*

"You're ready to deliver," said Dr. Ingalls. "How about coming in on Thursday?"

"How about Friday?" I asked. I was in no hurry.

"Thursday is better," he said. "I'm going hunting on Friday."

I began thinking about all I had to do before Thursday and our big day at the hospital.

Siri had just turned three in October, and after bringing her to a friend's house to stay for a few days, Paul and I were off to Abbott Hospital. The nurses got us settled in our room. Dr. Ingalls came in and with his usual no-nonsense bedside manner broke my water. I don't remember much about the morning. There were a few contractions but nothing major.

Three years earlier, after Siri was born, I had hand-stitched a picture of a lion to add to the alphabet display hanging in her bedroom. Now

I had it with me at the hospital as something to focus on when the contractions started. But it didn't work. All I could think of was the cowardly lion in *The Wizard of Oz*.

Paul was holding my hand. In our birthing class I had learned to relax and breathe and go with each contraction, and Paul was a good coach. But by noon things were not going as fast as we expected.

"How are we doing now?" the doctor asked. There wasn't much progress. "Let's try this next procedure," he said. The nurse placed two elongated pills in between my lip and upper teeth. I had to hold them there as a stimulus to begin more intense contractions.

"We could have gotten action started by giving each other some passionate kisses instead," Paul said, with that certain sparkle in his eyes.

I could hear nurses' footsteps outside my room and the occasional gurney being wheeled down the hall—another mom about to give birth. I could suck on ice chips, but it was difficult to be comfortable. When Dr. Ingalls came in again to check on me, I asked him, "So what do you think about these new techniques of having a comfortable birthing room with beautiful pictures on the walls and music playing, creating a calmness for the arrival of the new baby?"

He lowered his glasses, looked at me, and said, "What do you think I think about the new ideas?"

"Probably not much?"

"You're right. A baby comes into this world with bright lights and a slap on the bottom. Babies need to know that this world is not all tranquil and sweet, and they need to know this right from the start!"

Little did I know how true this would be for Maja.

A new mom really doesn't notice anything about her surroundings, and I wanted to concentrate on the birth, putting all my energy into the delivery of a new little one. Time goes by unnoticed in those hours of counting contractions. But I was finally dilated to the correct number of centimeters. I remember being wheeled into the delivery room with Paul at my side. There were at least ten people waiting in there. I knew Maja's birth would be special. When Siri was born, only Dr. Ingalls,

Paul, a coaching nurse, and the anesthesiologist attended. This time it was explained to me that each staff member had also brought an intern to learn about the birthing process.

Everybody was ready for Maja to come out and meet her new family. Just at that moment all activity ceased. There were no contractions. It was as if someone freeze-framed the moment—but it was not just one moment, it was at least 360 moments. It was as if Maja and Mom were too shy to proceed. I remember looking around at everyone. The doctor was ready. The anesthesiologist was ready. The nurse-coach was ready. Paul was ready. All those interns were ready, but apparently Maja was not ready.

There was silence, and then I began apologizing. "I'm so sorry to make you all wait like this."

After what seemed like an extremely long time, on November 2, 1978, at 3:30 p.m., Maja came out for the first time.

What did I lose in Maja's first coming out? I was no longer home for Maja. I could no longer be her only source of protection in this world. I knew she'd have to learn to face the cruelty of others but also that she'd receive guidance from all who loved her.

The pain of childbirth soon passed, but the responsibility of caring for another human being was just beginning. What I did not know yet that afternoon was the joy and happiness Maja would bring me as we began her life's journey together.

Many people have used the word *special* to describe Maja. The first time she became aware of the word was when she was enrolled in the three-year-olds' Sunday school class. Each Sunday for an entire school year Maja was told that she was "special." Each Sunday the teacher attempted to teach the three-year-olds a new way they were special to God and their families. After the last class in May, when I came to pick Maja up from Sunday school, she had a puzzled look on her face.

I asked her what she was thinking about.

She looked at me and said quite seriously, "I have a question. What does *special* mean?"

I knew. She'd always be my special little girl.

What entered my life at Maja's first coming out? The joy of giving birth to her, whole new ways of loving, tears of joy and celebration, and the delight of taking care of a new baby, making this new little one feel comfortable and loved in every possible way. She is a part of me and always will be.

4

Coming Out to Dad

Closets are for clothes, not people. We must not hide our
gay/lesbian sons and daughters away, but love them, support
them, stand proudly at their side.

—Stella Marie Anderson, *My Child Is Gay*

Paul and I share almost everything. But since Maja worked up at
camp in the summer and then went back to Sioux Falls to begin
her senior year, there didn't seem to be any "good" time for her to tell
Dad. I respected her wishes, so I didn't say anything, leaving it up to
her to decide when the time was right.

Still, it was eating away at me. I finally called a friend who also
had a lesbian daughter. She listened and gave me some words of encouragement. She also suggested a few books to read. She sent me an
essay by Paul Egertson, a bishop of the Evangelical Lutheran Church
in America (ELCA), who had a gay son. Bishop Egertson compared
learning that his son was gay to learning that his son had died; he
described his grieving process. Reading about the stages of grief he
had gone through helped me accept that I had lost a daughter but also
gained a new daughter. I realized I needed to know more about this
new Maja.

Dare I say that, in some ways, it was like a death and resurrection?

While reading the bishop's words and talking to another mother of a
lesbian daughter were helpful, not being able to talk to Paul caused me

sleepless nights and tension-filled days. I felt a sense of urgency about visiting Maja together so I no longer had to keep this secret.

That fall Paul and I drove to Sioux Falls to see Maja. It was a tradition for us to go out to eat on these visits, and Maja had her favorite places to suggest. This time it was Spezia, a cheery Italian restaurant with tables covered in butcher paper and set with crayons so customers could draw while waiting for their meals. The food was delicious, with large servings, enough to take home for another meal.

Since we were early that evening, it was not crowded or noisy. We had time to just visit for a while and hear what Maja had been doing since the last time we had been together.

Our server, Tammy, was the picture of a Scandinavian beauty with her perfect complexion, blue eyes, and blonde hair cut in a wedge style. I recognized her as a soloist in the Augustana Choir. I also noticed that Maja's eyes sparkled when Tammy came to our table. I found myself looking at her in a whole new light. Did Maja have a crush on her? What's the newer term—*a thing for*? Tammy asked what we'd like to drink. When Maja ordered iced tea, I did the same. Paul said he'd just have water.

Tammy came back to the table with our drinks and the menus, large leather-bound volumes with pages and pages of choices. It could take a while to read. I watched Tammy walk briskly away, and my eyes focused on the waitstaff standing around in anticipation of more customers.

While we waited for our meals to arrive, Maja and I drew out our thoughts on the table covering. Paul sat back and watched the two of us sketching pictures and sayings.

Our meals arrived, and conversation slowed further as we concentrated on the huge plates of food in front of us. It was difficult to eat slowly because the food was so scrumptious. Their pasta sampler was out of this world—buttery, with more than a hint of garlic—and their salad greens tasted so much better than any that I fixed at home.

As we finished up our pasta, I asked Maja, "Is there still room for dessert? Could we perhaps share one?"

"Tiramisu!"

We scraped our dessert plates to get the last morsel of tiramisu. I could feel that this might be the moment for Maja to make her announcement. She took a deep breath and began with a determined look, eyes focused on Paul.

"Dad, I want to tell you something." Her voice was low, and I didn't know if Paul had heard her.

"Well, Mom already knows," she added, took a deep breath and plowed ahead. "Dad, I think I'm gay."

Dad looked straight into Maja's eyes and said, "You're kidding me, right? Another one of your outlandish statements?"

Maja shook her head no as she glanced down at the table and then up at me and over at Paul.

Her father half smiled. "I guess not." He looked once around the restaurant slowly, then leaned forward and said in a low, stoic-Norwegian voice, "Maja, you know I love you no matter what."

She looked so relieved. Her eyes sparkled once more, and I thought I noticed a spring in her step as we walked out of Spezia into the bright sunshine of a fall day.

We said our goodbyes, enfolding Maja in a group hug, and began our drive back to Minneapolis. After a while, I asked Paul how he was feeling.

"I'm thinking what a difficult road it'll be for Maja now. I'm worried about what might happen to her. How can we be there for her?"

"I feel the same way," I said, turning in my seat to look at him. "I love her so much, and it's difficult to not want to overprotect her. I'm still so bewildered, not knowing what will be happening for Maja in the future. I wish she'd told us at the same time."

Paul glanced over at me and said, "It hadn't even occurred to me until you mentioned it just now. It must have been hard for you not to tell me."

"Yeah," I said, settling back, "that was about the most difficult thing I've ever had to endure."

My thoughts returned to thinking about the future. How could I continue to help her? What could both Paul and I do to keep giving her support? Where would this lead? I could only look upward. I could only go forward and try not to be afraid.

5

Maja's Spirit

Be followers of God, as dear children; and walk in love.

—Ephesians 5:1–2 KJV

Maja Margrethe Kanne Knutson came into this world on a warm, seventy-five-degree November day in 1978. Her long name was a combination of my Aunt Maja, my mom Margrethe, and my maiden name, Kanne, as we had two girls and the Kanne name was in danger of fading away.

Maja was the baby of our family and was always getting advice from her older sister and parents. It was difficult for her to be independent. Someone was always there, telling her what to do. She tried to be independent from the first word she ever said, which was *"Mine."* Siri, three years older, would take toys away from Maja. Siri wasn't deliberately mean: she wanted to teach Maja how to play with them. But all Maja wanted to do was taste them. I, too, had an older sister, so I could identify with Maja when she wanted to be her own person and not just follow in her sister's footsteps.

Sometimes she did play the baby-of-the-family card. When she had lots of homework or a big project due, she complained for three hours, but when she finally got to it, she did well. Looking back, I wish I had just said, "Enough of this, get to it," and then left her alone until she was done. I was more of an enabler, and that has not made it easy for Maja in her adult life.

Maja had brown hair when she was born, but it soon turned to blonde. She had a bowl cut for many years, since I was the main barber for the family until she was in junior high. Then she grew her hair out. I enjoyed taking her to the beauty salon and watching her tell the stylist just how she wanted her hair to look.

Maja has hazel eyes with a mischievous look of wanting to play a joke on you. She has a winning smile, and her eyes are set in like her dad's. She doesn't need to wear much makeup: her eyebrows are almost perfectly shaped, and her complexion is typically fair Scandinavian skin that doesn't tan easily.

Early on Maja didn't always like what I fixed for supper. Sometimes she really tried my patience. There was a picture posted in our kitchen of a baby with spaghetti draped over her head. Under the picture was the Bible quote "This is the day that the Lord has made; let us rejoice and be glad in it" (Psalm 118:24). I used to say Maja was that baby in the picture. She didn't put the spaghetti on her head; I did because she refused to eat it. As time went on Maja became a good sport about trying all sorts of foods.

When she began taking swimming lessons at the age of two, she didn't like to put her face in the water. The whole idea of being under the water scared her. It was partly my fault. Siri had started lessons at six months. I had started Maja too late, and it took weekly lessons and lots of positive convincing from me before she gradually became braver. Years later she would not so much sail as perhaps paddle through the grueling and challenging American Red Cross Water Safety Instructor Certification, a requirement for a camp counselor job.

Maja, Siri, Paul, and I have traveled to forty-eight out of the fifty states during summer months and visited friends and relatives. It helps to have two teachers as parents. We have three months off in the summer to travel and learn about new places. It was a time for the entire family to bond, to help set up camp together, and to talk about all kinds of subjects, from the Bible to who wants to play another game of UNO.

Maja wasn't always happy about travel. Once, when she was about five, we were camping in Estes Park, Colorado. In nearby Denver, huge masses of foreboding clouds bent down to the ground, shielding the mountains from view. When we awoke the next morning, the sun shone into our tent and the sky was azure blue. Maja loved to sleep in even as a child, but I woke her.

"Maja, come and look out the window of the tent. You can see the mountains," I said. She stood up, looked out the window for two seconds, and then fell back onto her sleeping bag. I tried again: "Maja, look at the mountains." A muffled voice replied, "I already saw them."

Maja enjoyed the outdoors. She liked the wide-open spaces but felt hemmed in when we were in the state of Washington because there was ocean to the west and mountains to the east. It wasn't until we came to the middle of Montana that she felt better.

Music has been a part of Maja's life from the beginning. I sang to her when I was changing her diaper. At an early age she knew the words to many hymns and loved listening and participating too. Our family attended a wedding when Maja was about five. After one of the Scripture readings, Maja looked over at me and in a loud whisper announced, "Mom, that's First John four, verses seven and eight." The person in the pew in front of us turned around, not quite believing what she had just heard. Little did she know that those verses are in a children's song that quotes the Scripture passage.

> Beloved, let us love one another
> For love is of God and everyone who loveth is born of God
> and knoweth God.
> He that loveth not [clap, clap, clap] knoweth not God; for
> God is love.
> Beloved, let us love one another. 1 John 4, 7 and 8 [clap, clap].

Maja began playing the violin when she was in third grade. She had a good ear for playing in tune, but diligence with practicing was another story. One time, when I was helping her practice, she handed me the violin and said, "Here, Mom, you do it." Later she switched to the viola, which she still plays. It is therapeutic for her in times of stress.

Her aunt and uncle were both music teachers and two of her cousins were musicians, so we attended many concerts over the years. Singing is one of my passions, so I found opportunities for Maja and Siri to sing. They sang in Angelica Cantanti, a children's choir my sister directed, as well as church choirs. Our church's Cathedral Choir was made up of over one hundred teenagers, and they sang almost every Sunday at the nine and ten o'clock worship services. It was quite a commitment, but the words to those anthems are still in Maja's understanding and heart; they have helped grow her faith and guide her in life. I am thankful that Maja and I can share our faith in song, talk about our doubts, and continue to grow in our belief in God together.

One summer, when Maja was in high school, she was selected to participate in a string quartet camp in Ashland, Oregon. Her cousin Kirsten was the violist in the Cavani String Quartet and had also been her first violin teacher. There were twenty-eight participants, enough for seven quartets consisting of first and second violin, viola, and cello.

I hoped Maja would gain some independence from the experience. She flew out to Oregon with other musicians from Minneapolis who were attending the quartet program. I still felt reluctant to let her travel so far away from home, although I knew that Kirsten would be there as well as the other members of the Cavani Quartet.

From what Maja told me, I think the camp was a challenge musically for her. She also didn't find any kindred spirits there, except for the quartet teachers she knew through Kirsten.

More than a year later, when the Cavani Quartet came to play a concert in St. Paul, I talked with the musicians about their most recent experience at the camp. Maja hadn't attended that year, and they told me they missed Maja's spirit. I talked to each member individually and was surprised that they all said the same thing.

I have always enjoyed Maja's sense of humor and admired the empathy and compassion she feels for others. Siri has said many times that Maja knows her so well that she can almost read her mind. In her younger years Maja had some funny sayings and facial expressions that made us all laugh when things got tense. She could even make her mouth into the shape of a canoe. She's also a gifted listener, and she'll say just the right words to help someone feel better.

My facial expression usually gives my emotions away. When I'm angry or disappointed, Maja will notice and ask me about it, getting me to talk it out and clarify what my feelings are. If I'm frustrated about something, I will withdraw from the situation. I remember one time I went out to the front porch to simmer down. Maja waited awhile and then came out to find me. She wasn't the source of my frustration, but she helped me talk about my feelings, and she had some good ideas for me. Sometimes she just knows the right words to say.

Maja continued her love of the outdoors and applied to work at Wilderness Canoe Base during the summer of 1999, between her sophomore and junior years of college. On July 4 the phone rang just as Paul and I were leaving the house. We were already running late. I only caught part of the conversation and heard Paul say, "Thanks for letting us know. I'm relieved to hear everyone's okay."

Paul's tone of voice told me something was wrong. I knew something had happened to Maja or Siri. He came out the back door and said, "That was Christa on the phone."

"Christa?"

"From Wilderness Canoe Base."

"What'd she want?"

"To let us know that everyone was safe after the storm. Maja's okay."

"What did she mean, 'Maja's okay'?" Now I was beginning to panic.

In his usual way Paul tried to calm me down. "Christa told me there was a big storm in the area yesterday."

"We didn't hear anything about that last night."

"I guess since all the telephone lines were down, there were no reports on the storm. A few of the Wilderness Canoe Base staff managed to get to town to call the families."

I felt queasy thinking of Maja in the storm, but I breathed a sigh of relief that no one had been hurt. Wilderness Canoe Base is a Lutheran camp located in the Boundary Waters Canoe Area in northern

Minnesota. When we finally were able to talk to Maja directly, she told us what happened the day of the blowdown.

It was a calm, sunny Sunday afternoon. The staff was eating lunch in the dining hall. Most of the campers had gone back to civilization that morning. Then the wind began to blow.

The gusts grew intense and violent. Trees snapped in half, their branches falling in every direction. It wasn't a tornado but straight-line winds. Within an hour the storm had moved on through the wilderness, blowing down everything in its path.

All the paths to the cabins at the camp were blocked with tree branches and debris. Maja told us later, "It took two days before we finally cleared a path to get back to my cabin. I really didn't know what to do. So I tried to keep some order in the chaos. Lots of staffers cleared brush. Others went in search of the one canoe-trip group that was still out on the trail. We prayed a lot too. I mostly did little jobs, like sweeping the dining room floor and helping with meals. I wasn't leading the pack but just followed orders. I really didn't think I did much to help."

About three weeks after the blowdown, Paul and I drove to Wilderness Canoe Base to visit Maja. Since the base is located on two separate islands, everyone canoes from the mainland to get there. One of the base staff members helped us paddle over to the island. She asked, "Who are you coming to visit?"

"Our daughter Maja."

"Oh, Maja. She taught me a new song last night."

"Really, which song was it?"

"Beautiful Savior." I almost started singing the hymn. The second verse was especially inspiring in the aftermath of the blowdown:

> Fair are the meadows,
> Fair are the woodlands,
> Robed in flow'rs of blooming spring;
> Jesus is fairer, Jesus is purer,
> He makes our sorrowing spirit sing.

I was quite surprised that she hadn't known the song, but I was also proud of Maja. She has a wide repertoire of songs, from Bach to folk to pop to hymns.

When we arrived at camp, we learned that Maja was in sickbay, and my worry button kicked in. Apparently she had just found out that she was allergic to mango skin. The night before we arrived someone had donated some mangoes as a snack, and she had jokingly picked one out, bit into it, and said, "This one's mine." She had an immediate allergic reaction, and the nurse treated it with Benadryl, which made her extremely drowsy and not herself.

Wilderness Canoe Base was sixty miles from the nearest town with health facilities. I was worried. What if the allergic reaction had been worse?

Maja looked tired and rather weak to me. I wanted to assume that mothering role, to soothe and protect her, and even bring her home. She told me she loved being out in the wilderness, but when the blow-down happened, everything changed. There was no back to normal; all plans had been torn apart, just like the trees in the storm.

At the end of the summer each staff member had an exit interview with the camp director. Maja told us she was so surprised to hear Jim say how much he appreciated what she had done during the blowdown. Apparently he had noticed that while everyone else was racing around, trying to solve new problems, she had stayed behind to clean the floor in the dining hall and do other chores that had been totally forgotten. She did other staff members' assigned jobs for them. In this way she had helped maintain some stability. Not everyone had noticed, but the director acknowledged and thanked her. As her proud mom, I have told this story of Maja's adventure many times. Once again, Maja's spirit came shining through.

My Enlightenment

I pray that the eyes of your heart may be enlightened, so that
you will know what is the hope of God's calling.
—Ephesians 1:18 NASU

After that first afternoon when Maja told me she was lesbian, the
image of falling out of a canoe into ice-cold water kept appearing
in my thoughts. Would I be able to find my paddle and get back into the
canoe with Maja? Would we be safe and calm again, as Douglas Wood
writes, gliding on "with the paddle whispering"? Maja was the one who
had learned how to rescue others. Would she be saving me this time?

Some people in my life heard the story of Maja and supported me.
Their empathy and concern were so welcome. They listened and com-
forted. But there were times over those months when I discovered that
some of my friends wouldn't support me. They had been taught that
being gay was a sin. The Bible said so. They chose not to bring up the
subject of Maja being lesbian because they didn't want to alienate me. I
felt frustrated as I tried to find a way to reach them. There was a parting
of the ways, and these friendships faded.

I wished their responses had all been like my friend Judy's. Unconditional love for my family always came first with her. She told me she
didn't understand this whole thing about being lesbian, but she knew
Maja and loved her. Around other friends and people I knew, I felt that
I had been put in the closet too. We Scandinavians find it hard to talk

openly about uncomfortable subjects. I didn't think I knew enough to speak out in a gentle way, to inform and not just be frustrated at how uninformed some friends could be. When they abandoned me, I was disappointed, but I knew their friendship was not unconditional and I shouldn't use my energy to keep the friendship intact.

Over the course of my life I've encountered many people with stories that ultimately intertwined with mine. Some offered loving concern and advice. I believe these people were placed in my path to help me accept and be supportive of Maja. When I close my eyes and think back, I envision a long road with events and people lined up along it. Sometimes the path had unexpected curves and steep hills to climb. Sometimes I felt as if I were walking through a maze. But then I would reconnect with a friend who helped guide me along the path and pushed me up those hills.

The first time I learned a friend of mine was gay was back in 1988. Paul and I were traveling with our daughters to New York City. I had contacted a high school friend to let her know we were coming, and she invited us to meet her for lunch.

When I talked to her by phone to decide where to go for lunch, she told me about her commitment to her "roommate." She wanted me to meet her. I thought to myself, *"Commitment to my roommate"? Now what does that mean?* We agreed to meet at Artie's, Marcy's favorite deli. Marcy and Diane had nicknamed it Arteries. It was within walking distance of their apartment.

Being in New York City with our children sparked an adventure in itself. We took the subways and buses. The crowds of people intrigued our daughters. And New Yorkers seemed to be intrigued by Maja and Siri, ages six and nine, who at the time had very blonde hair, blue eyes, and Scandinavian features. Strangers smiled at our family, and as we were getting off the bus, two teenage girls stood up, bowed slightly, and offered each of our girls a wrapped piece of candy. What a nice surprise! Maja and Siri took the candy, smiled, and said, "Thank you," in unison as we stepped off the bus.

"New York's a friendly place," Paul commented.

"Guess so," I agreed, taking the girls by the hand.

I recognized Marcy immediately. She was waiting for us as we approached the deli. Her curly black hair was cut short. She was thinner than the last time I'd seen her; with a purse on a long strap slung over one shoulder, she wore pants and a light-blue shirt and looked rather boyish.

How fun to see Marcy again and remember our times together in high school! I felt that her roommate, Diane, was a kindred spirit right away, and when we found out she was from Anoka, Minnesota, not far from Minneapolis, that clinched it.

Marcy told me that back in those high school years she had adopted our family as her own. We had been so kind to her and welcomed her in with our Danish hospitality. Now I could see how happy Marcy and Diane seemed to be. They kidded each other, laughed together, and even finished each other's sentences.

Renewing my friendship with Marcy made me think back to those years in the early 1960s, in Pasadena, California. I attended John Muir High School, which had more than three thousand students in just the tenth through twelfth grades. I enjoyed it because there were people of different racial, religious, and socioeconomic backgrounds. I liked getting to know them, being invited over to their homes, and learning more about their points of view.

I sang in the school choir and was chosen to sing in a madrigal group with sixteen members. We represented our high school at many events in the community. The group performed at meetings of the Kiwanis, Rotary, and Zonta service clubs in the city, but in those days racial integration was still not accepted in some places. I remember seeing only white faces in the audiences. I sang tenor and stood in the back row with the boys, and I enjoyed marching off the stage arm in arm with choir members of different races just to see if anyone in the audience noticed. There was something about that shock factor that made me feel I was making a statement of acceptance of all people as equals.

Humor at Muir was also a big part of getting to know each other. Many times we whites were called "fades" or "grays," with the inference that black was the right color and we had just faded. There was of course still some tension, but the principal created a group of student representatives from various backgrounds to help the entire community understand each other better.

My friend Rosie, who also sang in the madrigal group, told me about her visit to relatives who lived in the South. As she left for her trip, her family gave her advice about which bathrooms to use and told her to sit in the back of the bus. I was surprised. At the time I wasn't aware of how blacks were treated in the South. Rosie's story helped me begin to understand how unjust discrimination was.

In my teens I became more aware of bigoted statements made around me, and I found myself being an advocate for my friends whenever I could. In my senior year I wrote a research paper on the 1954 US Supreme Court decision that required the desegregation of public schools. I wrote the paper three different ways: first for my history class, second for a controversial topic assignment in my sociology class, and third as an essay in English class. In the process I learned about segregation and the civil rights being denied the black community in the South. One book in particular, *Black Like Me,* by John Howard Griffin, gave me even more compassion for my friends. After reading about the Deep South, I had a better understanding of racial tensions in the South and also in Southern California.

Tom was one of my favorite people in high school. He was our school representative as a foreign exchange student in Germany over the summer, and then he was elected student body president our senior year. He was a true student leader who also happened to be black. Tom and I had a special connection, and we even won a joint award for outstanding service from the American Legion chapter in Pasadena. I saw Tom at our forty-fifth reunion, and after I gave him a hug, he introduced me to his partner, Steve. It was one of my first encounters with a same-sex couple from my high school class. Tom became another person put in my path to acceptance first as my good friend at Muir and later as another friend who happened to be gay. I wish now I had taken time to sit down and visit with him for awhile so we could share our stories.

My parents wanted me to attend a Lutheran college. They also wanted me to experience living independently away from home. So I chose to attend Augustana College in South Dakota, with students mostly from the Upper Midwest; only a few of us came from as far away as California or as foreign exchange students.

Rural South Dakota was a new experience for me, a big-city girl, and I enjoyed being a part of a different kind of community. Because I was far from home, my friends and roommates invited me to their homes in nearby towns. I was also part of a Lutheran witness group that traveled to small towns in the area to present an evening program of songs and stories sharing our faith. Participating in these small communities helped me acquire more knowledge of an entirely different part of the United States.

After college and teaching first grade for three years I decided to be more adventurous and act on my dreams to see another part of the world. I was chosen by the US Navy to teach at Byrd Elementary School in Yokohama, Japan. In the late 1960s many US troops were stationed in Japan because of the Vietnam War. I accepted the posting, which gave me many opportunities to experience another culture and learn more about the Japanese way of life.

One night a week I taught conversational English to Japanese university students, and we learned from each other about different ways of doing things. At the end of my first class I dismissed the students, but no one moved. I didn't know what was expected until one of the students told me, "In our country it is custom for Teacher to leave first."

Wow! I left the room, and then the students straightened it up, pushing in the chairs and erasing the chalkboard. I felt so honored to be in this place where teachers were respected. In the class we talked about many subjects, including discrimination, especially against women. There were also many more opportunities to travel, to learn more about other cities such as Taipei, Bangkok, Singapore, and Hong Kong.

During the '70s I enrolled in a master's program in guidance and counseling at the University of Wyoming. Paul also attended the university, and it was our courtship year. I finished my degree, and we moved to Minneapolis and got married in June. We both returned to teaching for several years. Then Siri was born, and three years later came Maja.

In the late 1980s University Lutheran Church of Hope in Minneapolis, where Paul and I were members, was active in many social justice concerns. One of them was the church's acceptance of gays and lesbians.

The church went through the process of becoming a Reconciled in Christ church. This meant holding a series of Sunday morning adult forums to discuss accepting openly gay people into the church. Being in this movement means offering a direct invitation to gay people stating, "You are welcome here."

I was somewhat confused by this whole idea, and so were many others in the congregation. I visited with a lesbian friend and told her I thought our congregation was inclusive. Why was a specific invitation necessary?

"We just want to be sure the members of the congregation are really all right with this open invitation," she said. "We're saying, 'Do you really, really, really want me to be a member?'" She explained that gay people weren't sure they were welcome because traditionally Christianity has viewed homosexuality as inherently sinful.

I attended all the forums. One featured a panel of four members with special understanding of the subject. Someone in the audience asked one of the panel members, a pastor who was in his nineties, if he believed that being gay was from God.

"Yes, I do," he said loudly.

I learned this pastor had a son who was gay. His absolute conviction that "this is from God" helped me through faith by grace to open my heart. I began to know that I needed to accept the whole person and not judge any part of them.

Thus, by the time Maja came out to me, my heart had been prepared to accept Maja's whole self. Even without those previous experiences, my love for my child would have led me to support and love her no matter what. I was still startled—even shocked—by her announcement. But I accepted it. So many families reject their gay children. But I also knew I had to study up, learn more, so I could help my daughter.

Two former bishops of the ELCA, Lowell Erdahl and Herbert Chilstrom, wrote a book entitled *Sexual Fulfillment for Single and Married, Straight and Gay, Young and Old.* Their honest and candid writing guided me to a deeper understanding of human sexuality.

Since Bishop Erdahl had been our minister for ten years and had baptized Maja, I visited with him often to learn more. He could be so persuasive when talking with people who disagreed with his ideas on the subject of homosexuality. I asked him about the secret to his success, but he didn't really have any answers for me. He gave me a copy of a letter he had written to Minnesota Public Radio at their request.

> I now thank God for gay and lesbian Christians who have been my teachers. They have introduced me to a significant segment of humanity who, through no choice of their own, are attracted to, fall in love with and desire to live in life-long partnership with persons of the same sex. The biblical texts that are so often quoted say nothing about homosexuality, as we understand it today or concerning persons in life-long, life-giving, committed relationships. For them we turn to other texts such as Romans 13:8–10 that says, . . . "Owe no one anything, except to love one another . . . Love does no wrong to a neighbor; therefore, love is the fulfilling of the law." I regret my previous blindness and the harm I have caused.

I wanted to take the verse "Love does no wrong to a neighbor" and proclaim it to all, as Bishop Erdahl did. The Lutheran churches I have attended have preached the Gospel, "Love God and love your neighbor." But how does true acceptance come into our souls?

Another helpful book I read was *Straight into Gay America* by Lars Clausen. Lars, a former Lutheran pastor, was a staff member of Holden Village, a retreat center in the Cascade Mountains in Washington, when I volunteered there for a week one summer. He wrote the book after pedaling his unicycle through eight eastern states, asking the question "What do you think of gay marriage?" In the book he writes, "A gay unicyclist might understand more quickly than me how the danger of Virginia roads resembles gay America, how lack of safe space threatens life."

When Maja began to tell people about her sexuality, I could empathize with her, visualizing moments of absolute panic like those Lars experienced on his unicycle, unable to get out of the way of a big semi behind him. I feared for my daughter's safety and prayed countless times for her, as if I were on a unicycle too, riding in front of Maja, trying to protect her from all hurt.

7

Coming Out to Siri

With my voice I cry out to the Lord . . .
When my spirit faints within me, you know my way.

—Psalm 142:1, 3 ESV

I dialed Maja's phone number. In my mind I urged her, *Pick up, pick up.* Her cheery phone message came on instead. Even if I'm not talking to her directly, I smile when I hear her voice. I left a message: "Hey, Maja. Siri leaves tomorrow, so please give her a call."

After college, when Maja was still living in Sioux Falls, Siri had been living with us. Now she was about to leave for a five-month stay in the Czech Republic in community with other Christian young people.

When Maja called back, Siri was in her room, packing. One thousand origami peace cranes encircled the room where the wall met the ceiling. Siri and Maja had folded the cranes together years earlier after hearing the story of the little girl in Japan who attempted to fold a thousand cranes to have her wish to live granted.

I handed Siri the phone. I knew this was going to be difficult for her. She didn't have a clue what was coming. I gently closed her door and went into our bedroom to be nearby in case she needed me.

A few moments later I heard Siri wailing in pain. My first thought was to go into her room, to hold and console her and perhaps sit in the rocking chair one more time and wail together. My hand was on the doorknob, but I waited. Eventually she stopped sobbing. There was silence. I heard the beep of the phone being disconnected.

I knocked softly and then opened the door. Siri was standing in the middle of the room, gazing straight ahead. I prayed that I could find the right words of comfort. We sat down on the bed amid the chaos of packing. I put my arm around her. I tried to describe what I had felt when Maja came out to me. Siri said little and seemed preoccupied. Her face didn't reveal her thoughts, so I finally asked if I could share the pamphlet on grieving I had received when I first found out about Maja. I wasn't sure if it would help, but I didn't know what else to do. My own words of comfort seemed so inadequate. She nodded, and we sat there together, my arm still around her. I began reading.

In times of stress Siri pulls back into a shell. She has often told me she needs time to think and process, so I knew no words I could say would be helpful. Eventually I left her to finish packing, knowing she wouldn't have another chance to talk to Maja before she left. As Maja's older sister, Siri had always played the role of protector, and now she was going away with this news in her heart.

While Siri was in the Czech Republic, she didn't have easy access to a phone or a computer. We didn't have a chance to talk about Maja coming out. The subject didn't come up in letters or e-mails. And besides, I never felt there was enough time to talk about it.

After Siri's return, whenever Maja was home for a visit, Maja told me she didn't want her older sister to come with advice about changing, about rethinking that she was gay. I didn't want to interfere because I thought my daughters needed to talk about Maja being lesbian, but I didn't overhear any of their conversations. Still, I was in protective-mom mode for Maja. I didn't say anything to Siri directly but felt for my daughters as they tiptoed around the subject. Maja called it "the polar bear in the room." Unease grew between them. They could only reflect on better times from their childhood, when they would sit in the backseat on one of our summer road trips, bantering back and forth. Siri was always amazed by how Maja knew her thoughts almost before she did.

There never seemed to be the right time to sit down together and talk openly about our family and how it was changing. I wanted to use a positive approach. I wasn't reluctant to talk about Maja coming out, but I felt that Siri and Maja should be talking to each other. But they never seemed to be together long enough to have a real conversation.

Siri and Maja had always been loving sisters, or so it seemed to me. They didn't fight or even disagree with each other much. Siri took her job as older sister seriously. Usually she told Maja what to do, not always in a loving manner, and Maja, who liked to joke around, eventually did what Siri suggested.

Of the four of us in this family, Siri had studied the Bible the most. She attended the Lutheran Bible Institute. But at the time Maja came out Siri hadn't read anything on the subject of sexuality or being gay. I was the one who had been studying and reading and talking with other people, including Maja. I had also read several theologians on what the Bible does and doesn't say about homosexuality. From time to time Paul and I discussed what I was discovering from my research. He wasn't one for reading or searching out this kind of material, but he was certainly open to hearing about it. Paul has always been one to thoughtfully challenge biblical ideas with his scientific background. Our Bible study group had read and discussed the topic of sexuality and the Bible as well.

One Sunday Siri and I were walking home from church when she brought up the topic of Maja's coming out. "I feel that you and Dad aren't being supportive of my point of view," she said. "You're just supporting Maja." I could hear sadness in her voice.

I realized that she was right: Paul and I had been so focused on Maja that we hadn't paid much attention to Siri and how she was feeling. Paul and I hadn't asked her, but she hadn't brought up the subject either. We were living in the same house but not sharing our concerns or even praying together.

I told Siri that I was sorry she felt unsupported. Putting my arm around her, I tried to reassure her that her dad and I didn't mean to make her feel unsupported. I asked her if there was anyone else she could talk to and confide in to get some of her feelings resolved. Siri didn't answer me, but she seemed to be thinking of someone to call. She decided to talk to one of her former teachers from the Lutheran Bible Institute.

Her teacher gave her some wise advice. She said she understood Siri's loving concern for Maja but suggested that Siri could become more informed on the whole subject.

Siri read Erdahl and Chilstrom's book on sexuality. She told me she wished there was one book that covered all the viewpoints. She didn't say much about her thoughts. I think she was fearful that I would attempt to once again persuade her in a different direction.

It seemed that the door to communication between my daughters was closed. They remembered their fun times together when they were younger, but they weren't getting to know each other as adults or confiding in each other. Since Maja was in Sioux Falls and Siri was in Minneapolis, there weren't many opportunities for conversations or interactions except during holiday get-togethers. Siri showed kindness to whomever Maja brought home during the holidays, but that polar bear remained in the room.

Eventually my daughters found a kind of resolution. With a friend's encouragement, Siri asked Maja's forgiveness for "big-sisterly" wrongs she had done to her. Initially Maja said she couldn't forgive her sister. But ultimately she asked for and offered peace, symbolized by a gift of origami cranes. Maja meticulously folded more than a hundred cranes and strung them together in hopes that Siri would hang them up where she could be reminded that her peace offering had been accepted.

Some of the tension between Maja and Siri seemed to be released. But I'm not certain how much the two of them shared with each other after that.

8

Confidence, Courage, and Character

Do not, therefore, abandon that confidence of yours; it brings a great reward.

—Hebrews 10:35

In high school Maja had confidence. She asked questions in class, played viola in the orchestra, was a member of the badminton team, and tried out for the school play. Sometimes she would surprise me and volunteer for something that I would never have attempted. She was courageous. Senior year she took an advanced English class. On her first paper, which compared and contrasted several books, she got a C. She bravely met with the teacher and asked how she could improve her grade. The teacher was quite surprised and told Maja that none of her students had asked her this question before. She offered a second chance: if Maja wanted to revise her paper over the weekend and turn it in on Monday, she would reconsider the grade. Maja got an A on the second attempt. I proudly told this story to my friends. To me it showed Maja's confidence in herself and her desire to learn and improve.

The school counselors who planned the National Honor Society Awards Program asked Maja to play a solo to provide music for the evening. When I first heard this news, I wanted to ask Maja, "Are you sure you really want to do this? You know how nervous you get when playing in front of an audience." But instead I asked her if she had picked a piece to play yet.

"I thought I'd play the Prelude from Bach's First Unaccompanied Cello Suite. I've been practicing that one on my viola."

I wanted to respond, "Are you sure you have that piece ready to perform?" But I just said, "Good for you, Maja, good for you. We'll be there for sure." I knew I'd be the one with the butterflies in my stomach.

The night of the event Maja calmly went on stage in front of all the other National Honor Society students and their families and performed her solo. I found myself folding my hands in my lap but also digging my nails into my palms and closing my eyes tight, willing Maja to get through that piece.

The viola sang out over the large auditorium. I don't think many had heard a viola solo before. When Maja dramatically played the last note and took her bow off the strings, she smiled, bowed, put her viola under her arm, and walked off the stage. I breathed a huge sigh of relief.

This "I can do it" attitude continued into freshman year at Augustana College. At first I got enthusiastic e-mails about her classes:

> My classes went very well yesterday. I know I'm going to like my religion class, but it will be difficult! My history class is also very interesting. There are also many nice people on third floor in my dorm. Chapel was good yesterday too! It might have helped my day go well . . . Oh, I wish I could type faster!
>
> Well, there is lots to do today and I hope everything is going well!
>
> Love you lots!!!! Thanks for sending me to Augie 'cause it's a grrrreat day to be a Viking!!
>
> Love, Maja Margrethe Kanne Knutson!

By sophomore year, things began to change. I noticed that her self-confidence was eroding. I knew that Maja was starting to question her faith. That so-called sophomore slump, when classes seem overwhelming and the energy from freshman year has waned, became real both physically and emotionally for Maja. Without a day-to-day connection to her, I felt at a loss even though I rationalized that she was just trying to be independent. But as the calls and e-mails slowed down, I began to wonder how she was really faring.

During school holidays, Maja came home and seemed in good spirits. She invited her college friends to visit, and we shared many conversations and meals around our dining room table. I felt honored that she included both Paul and me in the deep conversations she had with her friends.

One of Maja's friends who was interested in Eastern thought and Buddhism introduced her to meditation. At first I wasn't sure this was a good idea, but then I remembered a forum presented at church. A speaker on Buddhism assured us one could follow the philosophy of Buddha and still follow our own faith. Buddhism was more a way of living and actually could help Christians on their faith journeys. At one point, though, Maja made some comments questioning who Jesus was. I reminded her that Jesus's teachings of loving and accepting everyone sets the example of the right path to follow. I wanted her to know how important following the teachings of Jesus was to me. I wanted to remind her of what she had learned growing up in a Christian home. I hoped she would not depart from her faith.

Maja lived in the dorms on campus all four years of college. During junior year, her roommate's boyfriend stayed overnight some of the time, which was against the rules. Maja slept at a friend's apartment off campus on the weekends. I was so upset that I was about to call the school and let them know what was going on, but I knew it was really up to Maja to solve this problem. One of Maja's friends spoke up in her defense. He told the roommate's boyfriend, "This is unacceptable. You need to move out." I was glad Maja had loyal friends, and I was relieved the problem had been solved. Still, I worried that she wasn't learning to deal with her problems on her own. She had relied on someone else to resolve the issue.

That year, Maja also faced some painful disappointments. As part of her major in elementary education, she volunteered in classrooms each year at several elementary schools. When Maja asked one of her favorite teachers if she could student teach for her during senior year, the reply was, "Sorry, I've already been assigned a student teacher."

What I didn't know then was that Augustana's Education Department was on probation at the time and being audited to correct some problems. Maja's first advisor worked mostly with junior high school and senior high school education majors and was not familiar with the elementary education curriculum. Based on his advice, Maja ended up taking the elementary education classes in the wrong order. She got a truly helpful advisor in her junior year, but she still didn't receive the information she needed to sign up for student teaching in her senior year.

At least she enjoyed playing the viola in orchestra. But even then, at one concert the conductor did not acknowledge her as the first-chair violist. I saw the disappointment in her face as the director shook hands with the young man sitting next to her instead.

Her junior year did have a bright spot, however. When Maja got an on-campus job in the library freshman year, I thought it was a good fit for her. With her love of books, going to work was more a reward than a job. The spring of her junior year, the library staff nominated her for a special scholarship. The honor came at just the right time. It was a reason to rejoice and celebrate and come out from beneath the rejections.

Later, Maja told me she was surprised that she was selected for this award. She hadn't felt she stood out among her peers at school. That's how I learned that Maja and I had similar feelings of inadequacy and limitations during our college years. I had done so much in high school: student council, city youth council, choir, madrigal singers, and sports. But when I got to college, I didn't get involved in extracurricular activities. College was costing my parents money, and I thought my first priority was to do well in all my classes and learn the skills needed to find a job to support myself. I wasn't a leader in college; I didn't stand out. Maja did much more: she volunteered in classrooms, worked on service projects, and taught Sunday school. And yet she still didn't feel worthy of recognition.

At the beginning of November we drove to Sioux Falls to celebrate Maja's twenty-second birthday and attend the scholarship banquet where Maja would be one of the students honored. Since I had also attended Augie, it felt a bit like going back in time. The Morrison Commons building was relatively new when I attended back in the 1960s. It still looked new to me. The cafeteria was on the second floor, with floor-to-ceiling windows so you could gaze out over the campus while you ate.

On the evening of the scholarship banquet we all dressed in our finest—Maja and I wore dresses instead of our more comfortable attire. We picked a table close to the front. There were white tablecloths and flower centerpieces. The lights had been dimmed for the festive occasion.

I enjoyed talking with Maja and the people sitting at our table. I felt excited to be there with others, all delighting in this occasion honoring students who deserved special recognition. When each honoree's name was read, they stood, walked to the stage, and received a certificate. When it was Maja's turn, my heart was joyful. I felt like kicking up my heels and bringing out my lapel button that said, "Maja's mom."

When Maja came home for Thanksgiving her senior year—by this time she'd come out to both Paul and me—she told us about a special opportunity for student teachers to complete their first six weeks of student teaching in Japan. She was scheduled to do her student teaching second semester and thought this adventure would be a unique experience. She remembered all my stories of teaching in Japan and was excited about the possibilities. I wasn't sure this was a good plan, but I thought it might help her get her confidence back. It was a chance for her to develop her independence and prove she could manage on her own. Luckily, she had a good experience or so I thought.

After returning from Japan, she spent six more weeks at an elementary school in Sioux Falls. One morning we got a phone call from the head of the elementary education department at Augustana.

"I am not supposed to be calling you, as parents are not in the loop," he said, "but I wanted to ask you if Maja is stable enough to handle this work. There is a meeting with Maja and the teacher and the supervisor from the college tomorrow."

I was in shock. What were they going to tell Maja? What was not being said? My stomach was in knots, and my first inclination was to hop in the car and be there for support if she needed it. I decided that Maja needed to deal with this. But was she really able to? My mind raced, and sleep was not possible that night.

During her senior year, Maja had only been home during the holidays, but I hadn't noticed any side effects of the medication she was taking for depression. We thought she was seeing a counselor at school. But she was becoming lethargic, and one morning she didn't make it to her student teaching assignment. She didn't call her supervising teacher to let her know that she wouldn't be there, either. This went on for several days.

The committee told Maja that she wouldn't be allowed to finish student teaching that semester. She'd have to come back in the fall. I will never know for sure what that meeting was all about. I wondered if teaching was the right profession for Maja. But now I know there was a lot more going on.

After the meeting, Maja came home for about a week for a break. I took her to my doctor who assessed that Paxil was not the right medication for her, and she began to come off of it.

Fortunately, Maja had enough credits to graduate in education even though she did not yet have a certificate to teach. She returned to Sioux Falls and stayed there that summer to work. My heart ached as I tried to figure out what was next for my daughter. Why had she lost her confidence so dramatically?

In the fall she was told that her student teaching would not start until October, after the class was well settled into routine. Not long after she started, she was asked not to continue. Maja and her supervising teacher didn't seem to be able to work together, and the class was a difficult one to manage.

As a parent there was nothing I could do to make things better. I began to wonder if I had been part of the problem by always stepping in to help her and not letting her figure things out for herself. I also wondered if Maja's being out as lesbian had something to do with this rejection. I thought about asking if she could student teach in Minneapolis. One of my friends was a teacher and would have helped guide her. But this time I didn't interfere and hoped Maja could figure out her next steps independently.

Maja decided to close the door on ever working in a school. Her self-confidence was at an all-time low. She had a college diploma in elementary education, but without the teaching certificate, what could she do? She took a job of the type she had held when she was a freshman in college: working in a bagel shop.

Gone was the opportunity of becoming a teacher.

Gone were some friendships after she came out as a lesbian.

Gone was her college community now that she had graduated.

She was alone and struggling with the future.

I prayed that Maja would find the path to self-confidence once more and that she would have support from friends and family at this sad time in her life. Years later, Maja finally told me how scared she had been to go out into the world and start over again, searching for a new path in a world of work she knew nothing about in Sioux Falls, where she sometimes had to be closeted.

Eventually, Maja told Siri that she was interested in doing massage. Siri said, "Remember when you were younger you were always attempting to lift Dad, Mom, and me up? Even then you liked to massage the family's aches and pains away. Why don't you go to massage school?"

In January 2002 Maja enrolled in massage school. She had a gentle touch, and we all took part as she learned how to give massages. After she completed a five-month intensive program, Paul and I attended the graduation ceremony. The teacher made a speech, saying, "And now all those free massages you have gotten over the last five months will cost you money." I thought to myself, *Oh no they won't. Maja still owes us about five thousand dollars' worth!*

Maja set out in her new career. She kept her massage table in the trunk of her car; her plan was "Have massage table, will travel." In the beginning she seemed enthusiastic, but breaking into a relatively new field can be challenging, especially for someone with no experience in marketing and sales.

Maja also took a position at the YWCA. The hours were limited, and the pay was not enough to make a living, so she applied for a night job restocking shelves at Target. (She jokingly said, "I'm a stocker," as she followed me around the room, retracing my steps exactly.) Working nights paid more, but it turned her schedule upside down.

We frequently visited Maja in Sioux Falls, and she came home for the holidays when she could manage to get time off work. At Thanksgiving she came home on Wednesday but needed to be back at work at eleven o'clock on Thanksgiving night. She drove the five hours back to Sioux Falls and got there in time to have a short rest before beginning work. At three o'clock in the morning she hit that wall of exhaustion just as Target employees were gearing up for the Black Friday rush. As Maja headed to the bathroom for a break she began to cry. Her supervisor was also in the bathroom and gave Maja permission to go home and rest.

When she told me this story later that weekend, I was again ready to jump to her defense. Starting a new path can be so painful, and I felt her pain too. How many other young people are in this same canoe, just barely keeping afloat, unable to see around the next bend to where a waterfall might be?

Through these disappointments Maja still was willing to volunteer, now helping to teach English as a second language to adults. She started to visualize a different teaching career with adults rather than children. Perhaps this was the beginning of a new adventure. I hoped she had enough confidence to brave the unknown waters that lay ahead.

9

Cara's Christmas Visit

To everything there is a season, and a time to every purpose
under heaven.

—Ecclesiastes 3:1 KJV

I found myself flitting from window to window, looking outside whenever I heard a car drive by in hopes that Maja was finally arriving from Sioux Falls. I prayed the weather would cooperate. December could be a treacherous time to be out on Interstates 90 and 35, with icy roads, gusty winds, and swirling snow. My heart wouldn't settle down until I heard familiar steps coming up to the back door. Then I tried to be nonchalant about seeing Maja again for Christmas. But what a gift it was!

The house was decorated, with candelabra in the windows and my collection of manger scenes from all over the world displayed on every flat surface from the coffee table to the mantel. The dining room table displayed the red Christmas tablecloth, the Advent wreath, and candles all in readiness for celebrating the birth of Jesus. Christmas carols rang out from the CD player, and the scent of pine from the tree permeated the living room.

On Christmas Day the family always gathered at our house, and this year there would be twenty of us. My list of what food to prepare and when to prepare it grew longer, and my thoughts were spinning out of control. I reminded myself to keep calm. After all, the family would help and they were each bringing food to share too.

However, this Christmas would be a bit different because Maja was bringing Cara home for the holiday for the first time. I wanted to make her feel welcome and a part of the family. I had knitted her a pair of Norwegian mittens as a gift. I hoped they were the right size.

Paul and I had already met Cara several times. I hoped she would feel at home, as part of our family with all its uniqueness. Maja and Cara seemed happy together, and in the little time we had shared with them, they seemed to feel comfortable around us.

A car slowed down as I peered out the window again. Yes, it was turning into the driveway. Paul heard it too, and we casually began to make our way to the back door so we could greet Maja and Cara. It always seemed to take Maja a long time to get out of the car and come into the house. I straightened up the newspapers on the kitchen table for the tenth time in anticipation of their arrival. Finally the door opened and Cara walked in with a basket in one hand and her suitcase in the other.

The basket had a bow on its handle, and she presented it to me. In the basket were the fixings for scones. How delightful! But wait, she wanted to fix them for breakfast on Christmas morning? I tried to be enthusiastic about yet another job to be done in the morning when I needed the space to continue Christmas Day dinner preparations. I put the basket on the kitchen table and noticed that she had even brought clotted cream and marmalade.

I tried to rearrange thoughts swirling around in my head. The phrase I have used so often came to mind: "Surrender to surprise." I didn't know how it would be with two people attempting to cook in our small kitchen on Christmas morning. I knew Cara's offer was thoughtful and genuine. I told myself it would work out just fine. I was happy that the four of us would worship together on Christmas Eve at our church. I'd be singing in the choir for five worship services, the last one ending a little before midnight.

Christmas morning arrived way too soon. A yawn escaped me, and my eyes seemed unable to focus as I descended the stairs to put on the coffee for breakfast. The smell of that coffee brewing soon floated right back up the stairs. Before long I heard footsteps coming down. I knew it wasn't Paul. His footsteps were familiar to me. It wasn't Maja, either. She is not a morning person. So it had to be Cara.

As she reached the bottom step we wished each other Merry Christmas. Cara sat at the end of the table, and I poured her a cup of coffee. This would become a routine over the years, our time to talk one on one, to hear what had been happening, ask questions, and solve world problems. I'm not a coffee drinker, but that morning I was eating my traditional Christmas morning breakfast of julekage. This is a Danish treat: homemade bread made with craisins, raisins, and dried, candied fruit. I had toasted it and spread a thin layer of butter on top.

I then got out the baking items Cara would need to make scones. We chatted as we worked. Cara knew how to cook, and we managed not to trip over each other in my small kitchen. I asked her more about herself and also about how she and Maja were doing as a couple; I was curious but didn't want to pry into their private lives too much. We were beginning to build a mother /daughter relationship. I knew that her mom didn't accept that Cara is lesbian. They still communicated, but since Cara's parents live in western South Dakota, she hadn't seen them for a while. I felt sad that Cara had to carry this rejection. But selfishly I also felt glad that Maja and Cara could be here for Christmas.

Cara told me the story of her and Maja's first date. They went to a coffee shop and then for a stroll down Phillips Avenue in downtown Sioux Falls. Cara began to smile, and I wondered what was coming next. She told me Maja was easy to talk to. There was no awkward first-date tension. Cara started to chuckle as she continued. Maja was cold on their walk, so they went over to Cara's apartment to warm up. Maja was hungry, and Cara didn't have much to eat, but she offered her some cereal. Maja asked Cara if she had any fruit to go on the cereal, and Cara offered some grapes. Then Cara and I both began to laugh. Cara said she had never seen anyone eating cereal and grapes. I told her that sounded like something Paul would do.

The scones were about ready to come out of the oven, and I began slicing and buttering the French bread in early preparation for our dinner. Time was passing slowly and quickly at the same time. I didn't hear any movement from upstairs, so I assumed that Paul and Maja were still sleeping.

We sat down at the table to enjoy the scones with clotted cream and marmalade. It was still early, and it was nice to take a rest from the tasks still ahead. Cara was easy to talk to and willing to share some of her life story with me. I asked her about when she first came out.

Cara told me the minister at her church had given a sermon on how Lazarus had been dead but Jesus had brought him back to life. He had commanded Lazarus to "Come out." Pastor Don had told the congregation that everyone comes out about something in his or her life and encouraged them to be authentic. That got Cara thinking and being willing to come out to people. This was the first time I realized how important a different interpretation of the Lazarus story in the Bible could be.

Cara said that after several short-term relationships and coming out to her clinical pastoral education class, she felt at peace and happy with herself as she was, whether she was single or dating.

I heard someone coming down the stairs. It was Maja. She had smelled the coffee and was ready to have her first cup. Her timing was perfect: Cara was just saying, "Then six months later I met Maja."

Cara decided to take a shower, and now it was Maja's turn to have her morning coffee and scones. I enjoyed these one-on-one conversations, although that day my anxiety about getting all of the food prepared in time was beginning to kick in. Hearing Maja talk about Cara, I could understand that she was someone special in Maja's life. At times Maja shared her thoughts with me, and at times she kept them inside. I held back from asking too many prying questions.

After Cara shared her story with me on Christmas morning, I felt closer to her. Cara's willingness to trust me with her inner thoughts helped me to give her the love that she needed from me as a possible second mom. It also helped me feel closer to Maja. I knew it wasn't always easy for her to open up to Mom.

Cara's Christmas visit made me realize that although many of our family's traditions would remain the same, times were changing. We would continue the Danish tradition of holding hands and dancing around the tree, singing Christmas carols. But perhaps Christmas morning scones would be a new tradition.

10

Forgiveness Is the Final Form of Love

Clothe yourselves with compassion, kindness, humility,
gentleness and patience. Bear with each other and forgive
whatever grievances you may have against one another.

—Colossians 3:12–13 NIV

Maja and I were sitting in our hyggelig living room on the love
seat. I noticed Maja's serious expression and wondered what
she was thinking. Her mouth was set with a look of determination, but
her eyes seemed to be dancing. With a half smile of admiration and
anticipation I leaned back and listened.

While worshiping at Mount Olivet Lutheran Church over Thanksgiving, Maja had taken Cara's hand, slipped off one of the many rings
Cara always wore, and placed it in her pocket to get the size. Maja told
me she planned to ask Cara for a lifetime commitment sometime after
Christmas. Since Cara has some Irish heritage, the plan was to give her
a claddagh ring, an Irish tradition. Maja had ordered the ring from the
Irish gift shop in Sioux Falls, but it hadn't come in yet.

I knew this would be a whole new adventure for all of us, and after
a moment of hesitation I put my arms around her. I prayed that this
was the right decision for both Maja and Cara. I tried not to let doubt
slip in or to express reservations. I took my cues from Maja's exuberant
expression of love for Cara.

Maja kept Cara in suspense for more than a month, but one day in early February they went out to eat at their favorite sushi restaurant. While looking at the menu Cara saw out of the corner of her eye a fluted glass of champagne set in front of her and the waiter dashing away. Her first thought was, *We didn't order champagne. We can't afford that!*

She looked up and saw the champagne bubbling around a bright silver claddagh ring, and then Maja asked, "Cara Lorraine Schott, will you marry me?"

With tears flowing, Cara said, *"Yes!"* Maja came around the table and hugged her. Then they had to figure how to get the ring out. Cara started to take a sip of champagne, and Maja cried out, "Don't drink it!"

Maja called us and told us the good news. I couldn't help wondering what the rest of the people in the restaurant were thinking. Were they curious, supportive? Was there a word of explanation about what was going on? Maja and Cara told me that because they were frequent customers, the staff was gracious and excited to be in on the surprise for Cara. When I asked later about how other people in the restaurant responded, Maja and Cara looked at me and said they were so excited that they didn't even notice the reactions of the other diners.

Cara later told me that as she drifted off to sleep that night, she knew her life had changed in a significant way. She felt they were two individuals being knitted into one flesh. I thought to myself, *That sounds like something a minister would say.*

Maja and Cara's excitement of being engaged and wanting to shout it out to the whole world soon simmered down to a time of disappointment. Maja told me that when they showed someone Cara's ring, they sometimes received a puzzled look in return, as though the other person didn't know what to make of the information. My heart went out to Maja and Cara. I shared their joy and also their frustration with how difficult it was to communicate their happiness to others. It hurt when they shared their good news with people who responded not with hugs and congratulations but with stunned, uncomfortable silence and the inability to meet their eyes. They decided to find a more traditional ring set to wear once they were married. They wanted a physical, visible reminder of their commitment to each other and the life they would create together.

Maja's engagement brought up memories of Siri's engagement and wedding, of course. Siri and Dan's wedding was on a late September day, sunny and warm, with leaves at their peak in colors of gold, red, and orange. The wedding was at Mount Carmel Bible Camp, where both Maja and Siri had worked during the summer months when they were in college. Maja was Siri's maid of honor, and Cara was invited along as Maja's guest. Maja and Cara were in the early stages of their relationship then. Maja had many duties as maid of honor that left Cara to fend for herself. Still, during that weekend the two had time to take a few strolls around the camp, enjoy the beauty of the lake, and talk about the possibility of their future. My mind was spinning in many directions the day of Siri's wedding. I was overwhelmed, so I left it up to Maja to take care of Cara and hoped some of our friends would invite Cara to sit with them during the event.

That day was grand and glorious in so many ways. When Maja and Cara made their announcement, I hoped that their plans would lead to a similar day for them. I wanted to tell everyone I knew about their news, but I found myself sharing it only with those I knew would rejoice and be happy for our family. Some friends didn't know how to react, and some didn't want to hear about the plans at all.

I observed some of the most noticeable differences at my Tuesday Quilters group. We make quilts to sell in raffles that raise money for some of our church's programs. Our group of six has met weekly for about twenty years. We share our joys and sorrows as we work on the quilts. When Siri and Dan were getting married, the group wanted to know all the details. They even helped to stitch a banner for the wedding ceremony and purchased a gift. Siri and Dan invited them to the wedding, and they all came.

I usually walk to quilting with my friend Hollis. I told her about Maja and Cara's plans, and she was genuinely happy to hear about the details. When we arrived, we sat down at one of the two large tables where we work on our quilts, and I began to tell the group about Maja's news. Hollis was sitting across from me; she smiled, and I knew I had her support.

I wasn't quite sure how the others felt at this point, but the congratulations I'd heard at the announcement of Siri's engagement were missing. I sensed that some members didn't really know what to say and chose to say nothing in the response to my enthusiasm. I quickly changed the subject and realized that I wouldn't ask Maja to invite the quilters to their holy union ceremony. I now understood what Maja and Cara must have been going through as they told people their news, not knowing whether the reaction would be supportive.

Since same-sex marriage wasn't legally recognized yet, Maja and Cara were planning a holy union ceremony at their church. They were good at keeping Paul and me informed and asking us for guidance when they had a decision to make. They really wanted the ceremony to take place on the winter solstice. We teased them about that. "I know why you picked that date," I said. "It's the longest night of the year." Ultimately, they decided to have the union on December 15, 2007, since the solstice was on a weekday that year.

It was an especially difficult time for Cara because her parents refused to support her. Cara told me her parents wanted no part of her life. They didn't even want to meet Maja and our family. I became Cara and Maja's sounding board, with suggestions and ideas flying back and forth by e-mail and phone. Cara sent many e-mail requests for advice because I had helped to plan Siri and Dan's wedding. Sometimes as we communicated we came up with a solution together, which made me feel that I had gained Cara's trust. She was beginning to call me Mom/ Mary, or M&M for short.

Cara and Maja had a bit of trouble figuring out how to do the invitations. I suggested they could go to Kinko's; when they told the clerk what they wanted, it turned out that he was also gay. He was enthusiastic and gave them some new creative ideas. I was grateful that Maja and Cara encountered him and other people who were supportive and helpful.

Maja still wondered about Siri and whether she would want to be involved in the holy union. Siri and Dan were now living in Omaha, while Maja and Cara were in Sioux Falls, and the sisters weren't staying in close touch. When I talked to Siri by phone, she didn't say anything when I started talking about the union. She didn't ask any questions. I had hoped she would at least be curious about the plans. Maja had not asked her to be in the wedding party. I think she knew that Siri would have a difficult time supporting her.

When Dan and Siri were home for Thanksgiving, just three weeks before the event, I asked Siri to sit next to me at our piano. "I've just been playing this piece," I told her. "Would you be willing to sing this duet with me at Maja and Cara's reception?" I looked over to see her reaction. She was staring at the keys on the piano. "Well, maybe you better not count on me," she said.

Until then I hadn't thought much about Siri's part in the ceremony. When I started talking about plans, she usually became quiet and seemed unenthusiastic. I realized she was having a difficult time accepting this idea of a union, but I had thought she would still be there in support of Maja. I had learned not to push too much, so I said nothing. Siri got up from the piano bench and walked away, her long blonde hair streaming behind her.

The holy union was now only about ten days away. Final arrangements were being made, but in the back of my mind I kept wondering if Siri would be coming. I had not heard a word from her since Thanksgiving. What would she decide to do?

Paul and I were given two tickets to attend the Augsburg College vespers service at Central Lutheran Church in downtown Minneapolis. It was a time to still our hearts and enter into the church season of Advent, which literally means "waiting." To me, Advent doesn't mean waiting passively, but rather waiting in anticipation. Paul and I were waiting: for Christmas to arrive and the birth of Jesus, but also for the weaving together of Maja and Cara's lives. My anticipation fluctuated from high spirits to low and back again.

The Spirit of God was truly at Central Lutheran that evening. The theme for the worship service was That All May Seek Truth, That All May Know Love, That All May Have Joy, That All May See Peace. The last two words intrigued me. I wondered, *How do I see peace with all that's happening with my beloved family?*

One of the readings was from Reinhold Niebuhr:

> Nothing that is worth doing can be achieved in our life-time; therefore we must be saved by hope. Nothing which is true or beautiful or good makes complete sense in any immediate context of history; therefore, we must be saved by faith. Nothing we do, however virtuous, can be accomplished alone; therefore, we are saved by love. No virtuous act is quite as virtuous from the standpoint of our friend or foe as it is from our own standpoint. Therefore we must be saved by the final form of love, which is forgiveness.

Sitting there in that vast sanctuary, listening to college students' young voices proclaiming the message of each song from their hearts to mine, gave me heightened awareness of being loved and cared for in this congregation. Voices coming from all the balconies of the church and then gathering together in the front in one mass choir to sing the final anthem poured into my soul. I was calm and yet edgy; my skin felt warm and cold simultaneously. Yes, indeed I did *see* peace in a different sort of way, an inner peace, perhaps a light within me that could guide me forward into harmony and forgiveness. The message that evening spoke directly to my heart and soul. I came away from the vespers service with openness to whatever the next few weeks would hold.

As we drove home, I was thinking of peace, love, and forgiveness while humming some of the tunes from the service. But my thoughts kept returning to the upcoming ceremony.

"I wonder if Siri will be coming to the union," I said, staring out the window at the snowy streets. Christmas lights were everywhere, reflecting off the bright white lawns.

"Yeah," Paul said. "I wonder that too."

"She certainly hasn't wanted to be included in any plans. I asked her if she would sing a song with me at the reception."

"What did she say?"

"'Don't count on me, Mom.'"

When we arrived home, we found a letter from Siri in the mailbox. In it she quoted several Bible verses and then wrote, "I've decided I cannot come to the union. I just can't give Maja and Cara my blessing, and I know that's part of what the congregation says as a response in the ceremony."

Holding the letter in my hand, I sat down in my blue chair with a feeling of frustration. "She couldn't tell us this in person?" I said to Paul. "After all that Maja did for Siri at her wedding, Siri can't be there for Maja? This is less than two weeks before the union! How could she do this? Where is her sense of loyalty to her sister? She doesn't have to agree with the idea of the holy union, but she could at least be there as an act of love for Maja."

Anger, resentment, and grief enveloped me. I read the letter only once and then tore it up. "This is what I am doing with your letter, Siri Ann. I'm throwing it in the trash!" I thought about retrieving the letter, but I was too distraught, too disappointed. I wanted to burst into tears or hit something or just sink down to the floor in utter disbelief. I looked at Paul for his reaction. He put his hand on my shoulder in an attempt to calm me down. I could see he was silently empathizing with me. He has such unconditional love for both of our daughters and chose not to say much after my outburst. I sat for a long time, letting my mind and heart grieve over Siri's hard-hearted response.

I went to bed thinking about how I could change Siri's mind, but that hope was dim. How was Maja going to take this news? Tossing and turning in our four-poster bed, I finally fell into a troubled sleep.

When I woke up the next morning, it was the Niebuhr passage that I remembered and the word *forgiveness* that came to my mind first. Although it didn't take the pain away, it was the word I needed to understand Siri at this time, and focusing on it helped me move on. I was sad that she couldn't be happy for Maja. I realized that this was agonizing for Siri too. She loved Maja but couldn't support the idea of a holy union between two women.

I didn't have a conversation with Siri in the days that followed. Perhaps I didn't really want to know more. My heart was broken open once again. I knew it would have been difficult for Siri to be there, especially when the words in the service talked about supporting Cara and Maja. My head understood, but my heart did not.

Siri had also sent Maja a similar letter to the one she sent us. When I talked to Maja on the phone, she was angry and frustrated that Siri had decided not to come. But I realized that I had to let my own frustration go and not be concerned about Siri. I decided to focus all my attention on Maja and Cara and the ceremony plans. I didn't want to let my disappointment in Siri's decision take away from their celebration.

11

Behold! We Are About to Do a New Thing

I'm deeply committed to you and our life together, and that is
why I'm making this covenant with you before God and our
family.

—Maja Knutson

Cara's parents were not coming to the union, but her younger sister,
Miranda, flew from Houston to the Twin Cities to be one of the
attendants. She was the only one representing Cara's family—or so we
thought.

The following morning, with the car packed to the roof with wedding
stuff, including the cake and the food for the rehearsal dinner, Paul and
I, along with Miranda and our friend Charles, drove to Sioux Falls. I was
relieved the roads were clear and there was no snow in the forecast.

I had ordered a kransekage, a Danish wedding cake. It is a stack
of rings of almond cake, with a large ring at the bottom and smaller
rings added on top. With about twelve rings, their cake looked like a
tall building. Maja and Cara have often referred to themselves as Miss
Piggy and Kermit the Frog; they had found figurines of the characters
for the top of the cake. Humor, laughter, and gaiety (pardon the pun)
definitely were part of this celebration.

When we got to Sioux Falls, we checked into the Holiday Inn downtown. We found Cara and Maja, and then, to everyone's surprise, Cara's
brother, Tom, arrived.

I smiled warmly as I finally met Tommy after hearing so much about him from Cara. I could see the resemblance in the three siblings and the love they shared. Cara was clearly thrilled that part of her family had come to support her in this time of joy.

Maja's cousins had come from as far away as Seattle and New York City. Two college classmates came all the way from Norway. Maja's cousin Kirsten came alone, because her two boys and husband still had a week left of school before the Christmas holiday. She was Maja's honor attendant, and she devoted her entire attention to Maja. Since Kirsten was the first family member Maja came out to, it was the perfect arrangement. I gave Kirsten a big hug—I was grateful for her role as a guiding light in Maja's life.

On Friday afternoon we decorated the church. A friend and I had designed and stitched an Advent and Christmas banner for our church. I stitched a smaller copy of it for Maja and Cara. It looked like a stained-glass window and bore the words "I keep on Coming" across the second panel. The first panel depicted the Nativity scene. The second had symbols showing how God comes to us when we feed the hungry, read the Bible, in our baptism, through the Holy Spirit, when we help others, through communion, and in times of joy. The symbol for times of joy was two girls dancing together. It had become more meaningful to our family because of Cara and Maja. We placed the banner on a stand next to the altar.

Just before the rehearsal started I put the food in the oven, feeling surprisingly mellow for having to serve thirty people supper. I admit I was a little apprehensive because Don, the caterer as well as the pastor officiating the union, was at the rehearsal dinner. Would my humble culinary attempt be met with approval? After the rehearsal, my apprehension was wiped away when I heard Don remark, "This lasagna is delicious, and the dessert tastes divine."

Friends and family expressed their love and support for the couple in so many ways that day. There was a gentleness and willingness to help, and an upbeat, positive attitude that brought more tears to my eyes.

Several of the wedding party commented on how brave it was for Maja and Cara to be publicly having a union; it made them feel that this could be a possibility for them too. Cara and Maja were indeed doing a new thing.

After the rehearsal dinner we were invited to Cara and Maja's favorite coffee shop for a roast of the happy couple. To represent the family I got up and said, "Here are a few gifts for you two as you start down the road of life together. The first gift is a pair of fancy aprons that I have made for you to wear tomorrow at the reception. I wouldn't want you to spill on your wedding attire." Cara chuckled, and so did Maja. It was well known that in Cara's exuberance she would sometimes knock over a glass at the dinner table. Cara good-naturedly asked, "Have any of you been baptized by me recently?" About six people raised their hands.

I continued, "Maja, for you I have made a special corsage for tomorrow. When I shortened Grandma Knutson's wedding dress so Siri could wear it, I had material left over. So I made you a satin flower. I hope this flower will bring you a comforting feeling and remind you that your Grandma Knutson is with you in spirit."

Other family and friends gave loving tributes as we finished our drinks and the gathering began to wind down. I didn't sleep too well that night. There were too many details floating around in my head.

In some ways the union was as traditional as a conventional wedding, but in other ways it was unique. There was the hustle of the wedding party photo session, and Maja and Cara observed the old custom of not seeing each other before the ceremony. Everyone was ready to begin, but it was not time yet. So there was a period of waiting like the season of Advent. And at the last minute we needed to find more people to be part of the procession, to carry the cross and the paschal candle.

Cara wanted to use lots of candles for the ceremony. She had been an Episcopalian at one time, and Episcopal churches use them more than Lutheran churches. The Service of Light was at the beginning of the ceremony. We had a big discussion of what to put the lit candles in and finally came up with nine-by-thirteen-inch baking pans filled with sand. After Cara bought the sand, she discovered it was frozen and we had to thaw it out. As I told Cara, one of the themes of the union was "surrender to surprise." Like a mantra, I tried to keep it in mind throughout the weekend, and I found it prevented me from panicking several times.

We have a family wedding tradition of organizing a small choir. Twelve people rehearsed for an hour before the union and during the ceremony sang two songs, "Beautiful Savior" and "The Lord Bless You and Keep You" by John Rutter. Since there were enough sopranos, I sang alto. But at the last minute I developed a case of laryngitis and could hardly sing at all—another surrender to surprise.

Before the ceremony Cara stayed in a room away from everyone. I later found out how alone she felt, but at that time I didn't realize her dilemma. My mind was filled with the details and logistics of the day. Now I wish I had gone in and given her a big hug and words of encouragement.

Tom welcomed the guests to the union and made sure each person received a bulletin and a candle. A string quartet began to play the processional music. Three were from the South Dakota Symphony Orchestra, and the fourth was Kirsten on the viola. All eyes turned to the narthex of the sanctuary. Four ministers in their robes led the way, two from the United Church of Christ, one Episcopalian, and one Lutheran. The flower girl came next and scattered rose petals from her basket. The attendants walked single file down the aisle. Paul and I walked with Maja as far as the front row. We took our places and then watched as Cara's brother and sister walked with her. I turned to watch Maja's face as Cara walked down the aisle. She smiled, and I thought she was about to kick up her heels when she saw Cara floating toward her. Paul and I went up and lit the unity candle. The ushers assisted the congregation with the lighting of candles, and each person passed the light on until all the candles were lit. Then the ninety wedding guests came forward and put their candles into the sand-filled pans.

I had a moment of panic when I saw the fire hazard we had created. Each candle had a circle of paper at the bottom to prevent the candle wax from dripping on people's hands. Luckily, the guests realized they should remove the paper before they put their candles in the sand. Gradually a warm glow filled the sanctuary.

The lessons read were unique: "I am about to do a new thing" (Isaiah 43:16–19); Hebrews 10:31–39, about confidence and endurance; and then the Gospel. The wedding guests joined together to sing the Magnificat, when Mary magnifies the Lord after an angel tells her she has been chosen to be the mother of Jesus (Luke 1:45–55).

There were prayers offered for Cara and Maja, for the world, and for needs of all kinds, and finally prayers of gratitude.

Then came the vows. Cara and Maja had written their own.

Cara spoke first:

> Maja, I want to walk barefoot, hand in hand,
>> through ten thousand ordinary days.
> I want your face to be the last I see at night
>> and the first I see each morning.
> We are celebrating today what has already begun long ago.
> We met as two separate people and through our
>> years together have slowly been growing into one.
> Our ordinary day to day brings eternal joy.
> At our best and at our worst,
>> we always love, care, and support each other.
> I choose you this day and each day,
>> and I give you all of myself
>> to hold in the palm of your hand and the center of
>>> your heart.
> This is my covenant I make before God,
>> witnessed by all those who know and love us best.

Then Maja spoke:

> Cara Lorraine Schott, I am deeply committed to you
> > and our life together,
> > > and that is why I'm making this covenant with you
> > > before God and our family.
> I will be faithful, loyal, and honest with you throughout
> > our life.
> Let us remember this covenant we are making today to
> > help us meet any challenges that are presented to us.
> I love you, Cara, and feel blessed to have found you.
> > I will always honor and support you.

The pastor asked, "Who presents this couple today?" The wedding guests answered, "We do!" At this point I thought of Siri's letter and how she felt she couldn't answer the way everyone was expected to. I missed having her there, but I remembered that forgiveness is the final form of love.

At the close of the service the choir members got up and took their places by the piano. I could see Maja and Cara turn toward us as we began singing. By this time I could feel that my voice was almost entirely gone, but I made a joyful noise anyway to send Maja and Cara the message of the benediction:

> The Lord bless you and keep you,
> The Lord lift His countenance upon you,
> And give you peace, and give you peace,
> The Lord make His face to shine upon you,
> And be gracious unto you, be gracious,
> The Lord be gracious, gracious unto you.
> Amen

At the reception, Paul came to the microphone and said, "Maja and Cara, we have a special gift for each of you. We want you to know you are always welcome in our home. Here are two sets of keys to our house. Come over anytime. We will always be there for you."

The best blessing of all: I had gained another daughter—another silver thread in life's tapestry.

12

Cracking Ice

I just came in from outside and the ice is just right for cracking. Do you remember how much fun we had doing that together out on our sidewalk?

—Siri Knutson Drontle

When Siri and Maja were little, they used to love to run down the sidewalk in front of our house, cracking the thin sheets of ice with their clumpy boots. They loved the crunching sound it made. It was a contest to see who could crack the most pieces of ice.

Three months after the union, none of the ice between the sisters had cracked. I wondered if my daughters would ever communicate again. While Maja and Cara were in Sioux Falls, Dan and Siri were living in St. Paul.

Then one day Siri called me and told me she'd sent an e-mail to Maja. Later I got to read it; the subject was "Cracking Ice."

I just came in from outside and the ice is just right for cracking. Do you remember how much fun we had doing that together out on our sidewalk? We always had those big clunky boots on that mom made us wear, but they did do a great job helping us crack that thin ice didn't they?
Love,
Siri

Siri told me she hoped Maja would understand what she was attempting to do.

It worked. Maja read two layers of meaning into Siri's message. I was delighted. It seemed that my daughters were at least e-mailing again.

In June 2008 Siri's dance students were participating in a ballet recital, performing a dance that Siri had performed in high school. She rewrote part of the story to better fit the Christian emphasis of the dance studio. Paul and I had gotten tickets and then found out that Cara and Maja would be coming to visit that weekend and to go to the Twin Cities LGBT Pride festival.

Dance has been a big part of Siri's life, and Maja had gone to many of her sister's ballet performances. I called Maja and Cara.

"Hey, I know you're coming to the Twin Cities this weekend. We have tickets to see Siri's ballet. Would you like to come?" There was a pause on the phone before Maja answered, "When is it?"

"Saturday, the early show. Dan will be there too."

On the afternoon of the performance, as we drove to the auditorium, storms seemed likely. Looking at the sky's green tinge, I thought we might even have a tornado. I couldn't help remembering the 1965 tornado that had touched down not so far away from where we parked.

Siri's students performed *The Magic Toy Shop*. I could remember when Siri danced it. Now she was one of the teachers, and she had even adapted it with a new interpretation, adding messages of kindness and gentleness.

After the performance we all gathered in the lobby, waiting for Siri to come out. When she finally arrived, the family lined up to hug her. At first Maja and Cara stood in the background, but then they came forward and offered their congratulations.

It was gratifying to see the family coming together again and also to watch Siri's students come up and hug her. Siri held a bouquet of origami flowers, each on a long wire stem. She had folded one iris blossom for each of her students. Several parents came over to meet Siri's family.

As we left Siri to prepare for the second performance and drove back to our house, the weather still looked turbulent. I felt a bit anxious as we waited for Siri to return. At last I heard our back door open. "Thank God you're okay," I said, relieved to see her. "How did the second performance go?"

"It went well, considering . . ."

"Considering what?"

Siri told us that the tornado sirens went off in the middle of the performance, so everyone had to go down to the basement. Eventually the storm passed, and everyone went back up to the auditorium to watch the students finish the show. Siri told me that the dancers mostly stayed calm.

I wrapped Siri in my arms, saying, "I am so thankful. What a traumatic day you've had." During supper we all talked about the ballet and how much we had enjoyed it. The conversation was light, but as Maja had said before, "The polar bear was still in the room." The stormy weather had passed and the sun was out again, but I noticed there was not much conversation between the two sisters.

Dan and Siri went back to their house but returned the next day. Six people crowded into the kitchen at once to get the food they wanted from the leftovers of the day before. Six people around our small kitchen table felt somewhat chaotic, and I finally took my dessert out to the front porch.

The porch has large windows, although they only open halfway. The ceiling fan helps to keep the air circulating. On the wooden walls above the windows I had stenciled flower designs using the rosemaling technique. In the summertime Paul and I often enjoyed breakfast there.

This particular evening in late June was comfortable, and I could watch the sun setting in the sky behind the trees and homes of our neighborhood. It was quiet except for a few birds singing. We heard no lawn mowers or leaf blowers, and we were even spared the roar of airplanes landing at the nearby airport—the usual noise on Sunday evenings.

Eventually the rest of the family joined me, bringing their plates of brownies and ice cream with them. Dan and Cara sat over by the windows. Maja sat facing Siri in the middle of the porch, and Paul and I sat behind Siri.

Maja took a deep breath and said, "Siri, we need to have an adult conversation. I'm no longer the little sister, and this is who I am now."

All eyes were on Maja. No one was eating—I heard no scraping of plates. Maja didn't seem nervous or apprehensive. Perhaps she felt Siri had taken the first step by sending the e-mail.

"Siri, Cara and I are together now, and we need your acceptance."

Dan and Cara didn't say much, only offering a few gentle and affirming comments. Paul and I also stayed quiet. This was Maja's time to speak out. Siri listened and seemed to be taking it all in. I think she realized that Maja was not a little sister to be protected any more.

Because I sat behind her, I couldn't see Siri's face, but Maja seemed to be satisfied by Siri's reaction. As Siri has often said, "Maja is the only person who knows my thoughts even before I do." Siri looked over at Dan and Cara a few times, but she said little. Still, a feeling of peacefulness seemed to come onto the porch as the sun set and the light began to fade. It was good to know that the ice was beginning to crack.

13

Marriage for Maja and Cara

Make their life together a sign of Christ's love to this sinful
and broken world, that unity may overcome estrangement,
forgiveness heal guilt, and joy conquer despair
—Prayer for Marriage Rite in *The Book of Common Prayer*

Maja and Cara returned to Minneapolis in 2009 to take part again in Pride weekend. One day during their visit, as Cara sat in her usual spot on the love seat, Maja next to her, it seemed she had something on her mind that she wanted to run by me.

"When we get married," Cara finally said, "I would like to change my last name to Knutson."

I was quite surprised and responded in a neutral tone. I didn't want to seem overanxious for this to become a reality. *What will her parents think of this change?* I wondered. *Will they think Cara is writing them out of the picture?*

She continued, "I'll keep my maiden name as a middle name."

"Then you and Maja will each have four names," I said: Maja Margrethe Kanne Knutson and now Cara Lorraine Schott Knutson.

In the spring of 2009 we heard the news that Iowa's Supreme Court had ruled that the state could recognize same-sex marriages. Since Maja and Cara were still living in Sioux Falls, close to the border of Iowa, it didn't take long for them to decide to tie the knot legally.

Other than seeing pictures of the wedding overlooking the river on a hot August day, family was not involved this time. I must admit I was relieved to just hear about it and not be in on the planning. Still, my worry button turned on for my daughters as they again struggled to cross a river in a tippy canoe.

Although Cara was not officially a minister yet, I knew she had been doing some substitute preaching (called "pulpit supply") in a small Iowa town right over the border from South Dakota. She told me she really liked the pastor in that little church, and Maja decided they should have their wedding there and ask the minister to officiate.

The minister was delighted to be asked but had to get permission from the congregation to have the wedding in their church. Several days later, Cara got a call from the pastor with the sad news that the congregation had said no.

As they were telling me this story I could feel their disappointment. It was another splash of cold water in their faces, but they were determined to carry on.

They asked a friend who lived in Iowa and had been one of the readers at their union if they could use her backyard for the wedding ceremony. She said no. "So she could read at our union but didn't want neighbors to know she supported us," Maja told me.

The rejections that Maja and Cara face are challenging for me, too, as one of their biggest supporters. Their canoe is tipped over, and the cold water hits them with full force. My daughters don't share with me all the times they get tipped over. They know I will come fiercely to their defense, and they don't want me to get all worked up. I want to hold them, console them, and love them for just who they are. Why can't everyone else do the same?

Cara finally asked a cousin who lived in Des Moines if they could be married there. It was a larger community, and Maja and Cara agreed it might be a better option anyway.

Now plans were coming together. They first had to apply for a marriage license. I prayed for them on the day when they drove to the courthouse in a small Iowa town not far from Sioux Falls. When they got up to the counter and asked for the application for a marriage license, the clerk seemed genuinely happy for them. He told them they were the first lesbian couple to apply for a license after Iowa had legalized marriage equality.

After they were happily married, I did have one question for them.

"So if I'm going to send you a letter, how do I address it? Mrs. and Mrs. Knutson or Mrs. Knutsons?" I asked.

Maja replied with a joyful smile, "No, just Maja and Cara Knutson."

14

Ripples and Waves of Water

Marriage is like a canoe.
Handled skillfully by two people
It can withstand almost any storm,
And when the seas are calm,
It is beautiful.

—Paul A. Knutson

That first year of marriage requires so many adjustments. Merging belongings, finances, different ways of doing things, and division of domestic chores: all of these present new challenges. I got periodic updates from Maja and Cara. I felt honored that they wanted to let me in on some of their ups and downs. In that first year working together is sometimes challenging. There can be rough waters and calm seas, times of paddling together and times of attempting to go separate directions.

Cara shared with me what Maja did to show her love and calm the waters. Maja was always putting things together at work at Target, from bikes to grills, so when Cara brought home a grill she thought they could assemble it together. As usual the directions were not very clear. Cara and Maja ended up getting really angry at each other and frustrated with the whole project.

The best times Cara's family had together were around summertime grilling in the backyard. Maja didn't understand how important these family times were for Cara. She decided she didn't want to put the grill together. In frustration Cara decided to do it herself. She finally got the grill assembled, but the ignition switch didn't work.

Maja watched Cara struggle for days to get the grill to work. One day, while Cara was at work, Maja went to the store where they had purchased the grill. She got directions on how to get the ignition switch to work and figured out how to get the spark they needed. Cara enthusiastically told me this was one of the most selfless, caring, and noble things Maja had done for her. Maja and Cara were back in the canoe paddling together, and the sea was tranquil.

Cara dreamed of going to seminary. She tried to get approved through the Episcopal Church, but the committee rejected her application. She couldn't understand why, but she wasn't bold enough to ask for an explanation. Cara confided in me that she felt rejected by her church and reluctant to start the process again. She decided to apply for ministry in the ELCA, of which Maja had been a member for most of her life.

Meanwhile, Maja was a volunteer with Lutheran Social Services, teaching English as a second language to adults. She really enjoyed her work and decided she would like to pursue a certificate or even a master's degree.

At this point they seemed to be in a holding pattern. As far as I could tell, they weren't getting on with fulfilling their dreams. Now, when someone asks me to do something, I get up and do it immediately—I'm just one of those people. My family teases me about it, and when they ask for my help, they also suggest that it doesn't have to be done right away: "Later is fine too." In Maja and Cara's case I wanted some action, but I knew I was supposed to stay in a supportive role. Should I just sit back and wait? The answer came in an unexpected way, through a choir anthem. God speaks in many ways—if I'm listening.

I remember writing Maja a letter quoting one of my favorite choir anthems:

> Come unto Me and wait, for My time is not your time.
> Come unto Me and wait, and you will gain new strength.

Those who wait for the Lord will mount up with eagle's
  wings.
Those who wait for the Lord will run and not grow tired.
Be still and know that I am God.
Be still and know that I am.
Be still and know, be still and know. I say to you, "Be still."

I told Maja that it seemed to me they had been waiting, but God was giving them signs that the waiting was over. When were they going to act upon their dreams, make them become reality? God was showing them the way. It was time to take that leap of faith. I encouraged Maja to act on her dreams. I also prayed that this letter would create action.

A mother longs for her child to make her own way in the world. Maja was slowly making her way, but "Come unto Me and Wait" was a good anthem for me to be singing too. To be patient and kind and not grow weary when I could see Maja hesitating to leap forward and try something new.

While Maja and Cara were still in wait-and-review mode, I decided to attend a writing workshop at Madeline Island School of the Arts. Part of that workshop brought me out into nature and got me inspired as I sat on a sandy beach and looked out over Lake Superior. For me, that spot on the beach was one of those "thin places" where "heaven and earth are only three feet apart," as the ancient Celtic wisdom saying goes, but in thin places that distance is even shorter.

I gazed at the water and watched the waves crash onto the shore. The pine trees sheltered me from the summer sun, their scent wafting into my nostrils as I took in the breathtaking view: azure sky, billowy clouds, sun reflecting on the water. I followed each wave as it moved from left to right, spilled over, turned foamy white, and then crashed onto the sand and became more like ripples of water as each wave floated up to the shore.

Those tumultuous waves reminded me of our life's journey, Maja's and mine together, with ups and downs, highs and lows, turbulent times when the world came crashing down like a wave upon the beach. Water images swirled in my mind, first one drop, then millions of drops gathering into waves. I imagined that the drops included tears—of both sorrow and joy—from my journey with Maja.

Life came crashing down for Maja when she realized she was lesbian. It shook her confidence during her senior year of college, and though she graduated, she didn't complete her student teaching requirement, and her future plans evaporated.

Then life experiences mellowed out into a time of ripples and calmness, when Maja met Cara and they became partners. Life continued until another turbulent wave formed: they had life-changing decisions to make. Should they move to the Twin Cities to go back to school and train for new professions? That could bring more turbulent times, more waves crashing.

At the same time the ELCA had also been experiencing turbulent times, in particular with LGBTQ Lutherans. The church was struggling with whether to open wide its doors to let in pastors in committed same-sex relationships. Many LGBT pastors had been knocking on the door for quite some time. Their organization, now called ReconcilingWorks: Lutherans for Full Participation, was present at every churchwide assembly. At each they hoped the ELCA would say yes to their resolution.

I had wanted to be part of that process and attempted to become a voting member for the churchwide assembly that would meet at the convention center in downtown Minneapolis in 2009. Sadly I was not successful, but I followed the proceedings from afar.

At the time Maja and Cara were packing up to move to Minneapolis so Cara could begin classes at United Theological Seminary that fall. Before the move, Maja was interviewed by the Sioux Falls paper. She said that whether or not the ELCA tabled the vote to allow ELCA pastors in committed same-sex relationships, she was still Lutheran and would remain part of the church. Being a Lutheran was an important part of her life, so what happened in the ELCA at the national level was also of vital importance. For Maja this was part of her journey with God. She had a sense of trust, of letting go, having faith that all would work out. Her pilgrimage with God takes place in nature, in church, and in community with others. During all these times of stress, her faith anchored her. As Proverbs 22:6 tells us, "Train up a child in the way they will go and when they are older they will not depart from it."

I too am thankful for my faith and the strength that faith in God provides for our whole family. The seeds planted in Maja's early life were watered along the way; they've grown and become stronger.

Since Maja came out to me, I read Bible passages in a new way. For example, there's the well-known passage from Paul's First Letter to the Corinthians: "Love suffers long and is kind; love does not envy; love does not parade itself, is not puffed up; does not behave rudely, does not seek its own, is not provoked, thinks no evil; does not rejoice in iniquity, but rejoices in the truth; bears all things, believes all things, hopes all things, endures all things. Love never fails" (1 Corinthians 13:4–8a NKJV). I believe this is the gentle approach of love taken by ReconcilingWorks and others wanting to make the ELCA more inclusive of LGBTQ people.

The ELCA put together a statement that carefully spelled out Lutheran views on human sexuality. This process took years to complete. I get impatient and constantly pray, "God give me patience," but sometimes add, "*right now!*" Whenever I have been involved in the Lutheran process of discussions and conversations, hearing all viewpoints, I've believed it would eventually lead to compromise. I had faith that in the end the church would vote in favor of what is just and loving.

I had hoped to be more actively involved in this process. After all, the church would play a huge part in Cara and Maja's future. During the debate over the statement, I watched for articles and updates to follow what was happening. I even sent some of the articles to Maja and Cara. I felt like a protective hen gathering her chicks under her wings, but I became frustrated with myself for not taking a more active role in the process. I searched my soul for an answer. Why hadn't I taken that leap of faith? My mind came up with excuses, and yet deep down I wanted to be there. In my heart I thought I was an advocate, but my actions were not showing how I really felt.

The ELCA did more study on the whole subject of human sexuality and began forming its final proposed statement for the national convention. I couldn't help but feel apprehensive, excited, and nervous, always questioning. Because I was not a delegate I did not participate, but because the churchwide assembly took place in Minneapolis, about five miles from my home, I could almost feel the emotion and drama centered on this important vote.

The final statement identified four different points of view held by the members of the ELCA. They could not agree, and so they had agreed to disagree.

The first viewpoint was that same-gender sexual behavior is sinful and contrary to biblical teaching and natural law.

The second view was that homosexuality—even lifelong, monogamous same-sex relationships—reflect a broken world and that these relationships are not the same as traditional marriage.

The third view was that Scripture didn't address the context of sexual orientation and lifelong, loving, and committed relationships that we experience today. This view advocated supporting these relationships and surrounding them with prayer.

The fourth view was that Scripture didn't address the context of sexual orientation and committed relationships that we experience today. It advocated for same-sex couples having all the same benefits as heterosexual couples.

If I had been a delegate at the convention, I would have been in favor of the fourth view: complete acceptance and equality for all. After years of work, the statements attempted to say, "There are four differing views on this. We accept all of them. So let us move forward and keep dialoguing as our views begin to change. Each congregation is free to choose a pastor who best suits their needs. In these four statements all views are included and all people too. Let all the people say, 'Amen.'"

The day of the vote I kept checking for updates online. I knew the process that was taking place at the convention center in downtown Minneapolis. The resolution on sexuality was presented, voting members representing different points of view broke into small groups for discussion, and finally they all prayed for justice and the right decision to be made. The day before, as part of the larger process, the members had approved by a vote of 771 to 230 a resolution stating that they wanted to respect differences of opinion on this matter and honor the "bound consciences" of those who disagreed.

On Wednesday, August 19, 2009, the ELCA Churchwide Assembly adopted the document. The vote was 676 to 338, exactly two-thirds of the votes in favor.

Another event that day at approximately the same time created more ripples to intersect with those of the final vote. Looking out my basement window, I saw the sky darkening and turning green. The wind had stopped. In that eerie time, waiting becomes endless and fear sets in. The wind picked up again. Trees in our yard threw down twigs and a few small branches. Rain pounded at the windows in waves of water and gushed off the roof in torrents. For some reason, when the rain begins, I feel calm. I think that when it pours the chance of a tornado is diminished. As the wind died down and the rain let up, becoming more like ripples of water sliding in droplets down the windows, the sky slowly began to clear, and the sun burst forth. I could feel my muscles begin to relax. I hoped the storm hadn't been too damaging. How long had it lasted—ten minutes or an hour?

I trudged up my steep basement steps and turned on the TV to find out about storm damage. Paul and I watched in disbelief.

A tornado had, in fact, touched down in Minneapolis and hit Central Lutheran Church, damaging its steeple. Luckily, no one was hurt. In a bizarre coincidence, the tornado hit at the same time that the vote on the human sexuality statement was underway. Our local paper, the *Star Tribune*, asked, "Was this a coincidence or co-incidents?"

That evening, just hours after the tornado, we arrived at Central Lutheran Church a bit early for the convention worship service, which was open to the public. Being in this holy place again reminded me of the vespers service that had taken place there a few years earlier, when I had realized that "forgiveness is the final form of love."

We entered the large sanctuary with its stone archways and vaulted ceiling. It made me feel small and humble. The church was already half full. This evening there was such a welcoming spirit. Instinctively I wanted to go up and hug everyone, even those I didn't know personally. That's quite a miracle in itself, for I'm usually rather reserved in worship.

There was a sense of excitement, of celebration, of giving thanks, and of unity. It was as if the "And God Said YES" banners were waving way up to the church's high ceiling.

As the first hymn began, a procession of pastors and laypeople in robes and colorful stoles, including Mark Hanson, the bishop of the ELCA, made its way down the aisle. To be sitting in the pew among so many people all rejoicing in song gave me chills and smiles. It was almost impossible to sit still and not jump up to dance or clap to express my happiness at just being part of this moment. The congregation sang thanks to God with gusto and enthusiasm. I sensed some hesitation, though, a feeling of not wanting to be overexuberant or flaunt the outcome of the day.

Pastor Barbara Lundblad got up to read from Mark 4:35–41. It was the story about Jesus and his disciples crossing the Sea of Galilee in a storm. When she got to verse 37, "and a great gale arose," the congregation began to laugh and broke into applause. She paused, looked at the congregation, and said, "And I chose this text long before the storm of this afternoon." That got a great response too. She continued, "In all my years as a preacher I have never had this kind of reaction to this text before!"

During the sermon Pastor Lundblad pointed out that the motion to accept pastors in same-sex relationships had passed. It had received the two-thirds majority vote needed, not just the one vote that finalized the decision. Again the congregation burst forth with applause. What a feeling of joy, happiness, and love arose in the worship service that evening!

This meant that Cara and Maja were 100 percent accepted into the ministry of the ELCA. It was a time of celebration, a time of acceptance, a time of doing a new thing within the church. I felt like jumping up and down and clicking my heels together in joy.

To know that the Maja, Cara, our family, and the pastors in committed same-sex relationships had been invited to get back in the canoe after the storm, to experience that sense of belonging to a church that had compassion and acceptance for all, brought tears to my eyes.

Cara would be in the first class beginning their four-year master of divinity degree after the ELCA vote. She would be able to join the roster of ELCA pastors in 2013.

After the worship service at Central I could hardly wait to phone Maja and Cara to tell them about this amazing affirmation and acceptance of them in the ELCA. It had taken so long to move forward, but I still had faith that Lutherans would finally understand and offer unconditional love, as Jesus has taught us to do.

When I told Maja and Cara about the results, their response was one of guarded joy. They still weren't sure it was really going to happen. They seemed to want to hold back in case there were more disappointments along the way.

Sadly, many congregations have come into conflict over this decision, and my heart breaks for them. Over six hundred congregations have chosen to leave the ELCA. In congregations that chose to stay, members have left because they did not agree with the vote. When members of our congregation struggled with this decision and decided they would have to leave, our senior pastor gently told them that he understood, but that our church was staying in the ELCA. The policy of our church was to say a gracious goodbye and offer an open invitation to members who decided to return at a later time.

What I didn't understand was why the congregations would leave when their views were also included in the human sexuality statement.

It was up to each church to call a pastor who they felt was right for their congregation. But fear and misunderstanding were at work here. These members' eyes and ears were closed to acceptance of LGBTQ people.

How would this affect Cara and Maja? Yes, they were now accepted by the church vote. But Cara would say more than once, "I wonder if there will be a congregation willing to take a chance and call me to be their minister?"

"Things will work out for you and Maja," I told her. I thought to myself, *Cara, you are so much like me—projecting ahead, thinking of those negative scenarios.*

As I looked back on those eventful months from my spot on Madeline Island, gazing out on Lake Superior, I couldn't help thinking that perhaps the churchwide assembly became one of those thin places in time when the space between heaven and earth seemed only three feet apart, and it was easy to encounter the Sacred.

The waves rolled along as they do at the beach but came crashing down for some who were not in favor of this decision. Have the people who cannot open their hearts to accept pastors in committed same-sex relationships fallen out of the ELCA canoe? Will they reach for the paddle extended to them with love?

For me the decision created a time of being at peace with the outcome as the turbulence diminished and the waves calmed, becoming ripples on the sand once more.

15

The Maja/Mary-Go-Round

If you feel that everyone should be free to live his or her own
life, the safety net can never become a permanent solution,
because if you rely overmuch on it, then you're no longer
living your own life.

—Chris Kluwe

During the three years when Cara was in seminary, she and Maja
came over for lunch almost every Sunday after church. Around
12:30 p.m. I would hear a clatter and knock at our back door. I looked
forward to seeing them and hearing about their week. It was a time for
the family to get together—and for Maja and Cara to do their laundry.
It was a hyggelig time to slow down and relax before we all rushed off
again to begin the next busy week.

We discussed everything from politics to religion to work to school.
Sometimes we talked about what was new and positive in the forward
progress of the LGBTQ rights movement, but eventually we always
got around to discussing Maja and Cara's finances. When that subject
came up, Maja and Cara would give each other that knowing "here we
go again" look. Paul's voice would change to his teaching tone, and I
would begin to feel uncomfortable about the whole situation.

I studied Cara and Maja's faces to see what they were thinking. Were
they listening? Would they take our advice this time? Inwardly I was
saying, "Paul, stop. They have heard all this before." Outwardly I'd

slide back in my chair, thinking, *I'm always glad they come to us with their concerns, but I do want them to handle things more independently.* As Paul lectured, I began asking myself those same questions. *Where does their money go? Do they know how to keep a budget?* Part of me wanted them to write down everything they spent for a month and then see what they could actually do without. I wanted to take over their budget for them, but I knew that wasn't my place. Sometimes I wondered if they were hiding information from me. Was there something they didn't want me to know because they were afraid of my harsh words?

When Maja and Cara first moved to the Twin Cities, Paul and I offered to help them financially until they could get jobs. We paid for Maja's classes and Cara's books. Federal Student Aid money helped pay for Cara's seminary classes.

As time went on it became clear that we would need to support them financially for longer than we thought. There were many discussions about ways to cut expenses. They had been depending on their credit cards for too long: they only had enough money to pay interest on the cards most months. They attempted to make ends meet but couldn't, and then we would help them out. It felt as if we were all on a merry-go-round that just wouldn't stop spinning.

Maja had assumed Target salaries in the Twin Cities would be slightly better than in Sioux Falls because the cost of living was higher. That wasn't true. During holiday peak times everyone worked forty hours per week, but after Christmas everyone's hours were cut. Maja picked up hours when she could and even volunteered to work in other stores if needed. Salary increases were almost nonexistent. The bottom line was that not enough money was coming in. If there were car repairs or other emergencies, where would that money come from?

At one of our Sunday lunches Cara told us her committee from Luther Seminary would be meeting with her in the coming week. Each student had a committee to help them through the process of becoming a minister in the ELCA. Periodically they all met together with words of wisdom and support for the candidate. I empathized with Cara and felt those nervous tensions too, waking up around 4:30 a.m., my anxieties spinning through my brain like another not-so-merry Mary-go-round. I couldn't fall back to sleep.

After the meeting, we had an impromptu lunch at a local restaurant with Cara and Maja and asked what the committee had told Cara. Cara said, "I'm doing well in most areas of my work. I've gotten good reports from my teachers. I felt encouraged about what they had to say, and they were gentle in their suggestions, too. They did say I could use some help in one or two areas."

I reached over, put my hand on Cara's arm, and asked, "Do you feel like telling us about that?"

Cara looked at me and nodded. "One of those was finances. They could see that Maja and I had quite a bit of credit card **debt**."

I glanced over at Maja, who seemed to be listening intently while looking at us for some sort of response. I asked if the committee had any suggestions.

"They said **we could go** and see a financial advisor at Lutheran Social Services," Cara said. "They could help with organizing payments and also give advice on how best to move forward and reduce our debt."

I tried to keep my facial expressions rather neutral, but inside I was saying, *Yes.*

Cara paused for a few moments before she said, "I think we'll make an appointment. It won't hurt to check it out."

Maja and Cara talked to an advisor who worked with the credit card companies, and they were able to get some of the interest reduced. Then Lutheran Social Services took over the payments. Maja and Cara now had only one payment per month, to LSS. They were only allowed to have a debit card to their bank account. This was a five-year plan to pay off all their debts.

I felt relieved. I thought, *Finally the pressure's off. We don't have to go through those talks about money.* But I also wondered if Maja and Cara would have had these financial difficulties had Maja not experienced that traumatic senior year of college. I believe she didn't get her teaching license in part because she was soul searching, discovering who she was sexually, and on the wrong kind of medication. Of course, teaching jobs were difficult to get at that point, so perhaps I was stressing over something that would not have been possible even if she were straight.

One day Maja asked me, "Mom, how much do you and Dad have to pay on your credit cards every month?"

"Well, I pay whatever I have charged for the month. So I have nothing that I owe them until the next one is due."

"You mean you don't have any credit card debt?"

"No we don't. I pay it off every month. We have been fortunate too that there has been money to pay these bills, but we don't use our cards that often, and we basically only have two major ones."

Why didn't I tell Maja this earlier? It would have been so easy to show her just what our payment system was. I could also have pointed out that the interest rate on one of my credit cards was only 5 percent. Part of me was thinking, *Well, my parents didn't tell me about this. I figured it out on my own.*

Maja seemed amazed by this revelation, and I hoped that with support from Lutheran Social Services, she and Cara would learn better financial management. In the meantime, we remained their safety net. Our parents didn't have the money to bail us out, but times were different then, too. Or was that just something I told myself?

In the back of my mind there was still that nagging question: *How will they manage without us?* Just as we thought they were managing things on their own, we would get a phone call from Maja: "Um, ah, could you lend us some money?" So back on the Maja/Mary-go-round we'd go.

We were all conflicted. Perhaps I should have started a support group for parents of children in their thirties who haven't quite become independent. You see your child struggling, and you want to help them. Will I ever learn to just say, "God, it's your turn to take care of Maja and Cara. It's not my problem"?

16

Unconditional Love Arrives in Our Family

Dedicate your children to God and point them in the way
that they should go, and the values they've learned from you
will be with them for life.

—Proverbs 22:6 TPT

It was a fall day in 2011. The leaves were at their peak in reds, yellows, and oranges. The back door opened: Maja was lugging in her usual huge basket of laundry. Cara was right behind her with another one.

"Hey, we're here."

"What's in the extra laundry basket?"

"Clothes for a little person."

"Oh, can I see?"

"We'll get them washed up and show you later."

"That'll be fun," I said. "I haven't really gotten into the clothes-buying spirit yet. Can't really imagine myself as a grandma, either."

Paul just looked on and smiled. We were both still wondering if the new little one would be a girl or a boy.

I thought it was a girl—something Siri said made me think that. Once or twice she referred to the baby as "she" and then quickly added "he" to the conversation. Siri and Dan knew but didn't want to tell anyone until the baby was born.

"Have you two about finished getting your clothes sorted? Lunch is ready anytime you are."

It was our usual family Sunday lunch around the dining room table. Cara and Maja sat across from me, and Paul sat at the end, facing the windows. We tended to sit at one end of the table because the other end was covered with books, mail, and projects I was working on.

The conversation came around again to the new baby, due to arrive sometime in December. "I'm so excited," Maja said. "It'll be fun to see Siri and Dan as new parents and you two as grandparents."

There was a lull in the conversation as we sipped our coffee and thought about that time ahead. I looked over at Cara and noticed her coffee cup was too full again. I was always concerned that she would spill, and on my clean tablecloth, too. But today she was concentrating on her thoughts. She said, "I keep wondering if we'll get to be the aunties. What will Siri think about us being involved, especially me?"

There was another silence. Cara and Maja both looked thoughtful as they stirred cream into their coffee. Paul's brow had furrowed, the look he gets when he's deep in thought.

I was thinking, *I'm sure Siri will be glad to have help with the baby—at least, I think she will. She hasn't raised this issue with us. I know her genuine loving spirit, and I think she won't disappoint Maja and Cara.*

Finally I said, "I guess we'll just have to wait and see and hope for the best. I think Siri will need both you and Maja to be in her baby's life."

Maja replied, "We'll have such fun singing to the baby and just holding her or him."

Did I detect a slight pause before Maja said "him"? Does she know it's a girl?

Cara nodded in agreement, but she kept her eyes focused on her coffee cup.

One December afternoon our phone rang. Paul was up in his office, staring at his computer screen, surrounded by his stacks of papers and books. He usually answers the phone on about the third ring. I tend to ignore phone calls, as so many times it's just some organization calling to ask for money. I was downstairs in the TV room, sitting in my red chair with the leather straps and doing some knitting. Paul casually walked in and said, "Siri and Dan had the baby." I was so surprised. I looked at him and blinked twice as if I were in some sort of time warp. Had I heard him correctly?

"What did you say?"

"Siri and Dan had the baby."

"Is it a boy or a girl? How much does the baby weigh? What's the baby's name? Have they called Maja and Cara yet?"

"Oh, I didn't ask."

"You didn't ask?" I took a deep breath. "Call Dan back and ask!"

Paul dutifully went back out to the phone in the kitchen and called Dan on his cell, then came back and reported, "It's a girl, twenty inches long, seven pounds, ten ounces, but they haven't picked out a name. And Dan just called Maja and Cara."

"Can we go right now and see the baby?"

"Dan asked that we wait until after three o'clock this afternoon so they will be settled in their room. They're still in the delivery room."

Paul and I arrived at the hospital around three. Not seeing anyone at the reception desk, we went into the birth center and asked for Siri and Dan. It was a quiet place with a few muffled voices and cries from newborns in distant rooms. We waited a few minutes, and Dan came out to greet us. He was smiling, and his eyes looked tired but also had a certain twinkle. After the ritual washing of hands, we followed him down the hall.

He was clearly excited to introduce us to our first grandchild. As we entered the room, we saw the baby resting on Siri's chest. Baby and Mom silhouetted in the dim light looked like a portrait of the Madonna and child. The baby had reddish-blonde hair, just like Siri and Dan when they were born. I thought she looked like both parents, but she had Dan's eyes.

When Dan called Cara and Maja, Cara took the call. Maja was at work and would not be home until 11:00 p.m. They were so excited and planned to meet their new niece the next day after work. Cara was still wondering if she would be accepted as the aunt. But she and Maja talked about all the plans they had for the new baby, how they hoped to be number one on the list when Siri and Dan needed a babysitter. As they drove to the hospital, they continued to wonder. All sorts of questions came up: Whom will the baby look like? What must it feel like to become a parent? Will we be parents in the future too? But that same question kept coming back. Will we really be accepted as the aunties?

They told me later that as they walked into the hospital for their very first meeting with their niece, they still felt nervous about how that first encounter would go. They hung onto their gifts tightly and walked slowly down the hall. The hall seemed to get longer and wider as they approached the room assigned to Siri. When they reached the room, Siri was holding the baby. She saw them and said in a cheerful voice, "And look, here come Auntie Maja and Auntie Cara." What a relief! Dan took pictures of each aunt holding the baby. Those photos are the first ones in Grandma's brag book. My grandchild's birth seemed to be changing things.

A few days later we had a big party to celebrate Paul receiving his PhD from the University of Minnesota. About forty friends helped us celebrate with vanilla frozen yogurt hot-fudge sundaes, one of Paul's favorite desserts.

When Siri and Dan arrived with our new granddaughter, the party had a second honored guest. After introducing baby Anastasia Elise Drontle, Siri realized how tired she was. Her old room was calling her, but before she could sleep, Siri wanted to make sure her child would be in good hands. Siri walked over to where Cara was sitting on the window seat, Maja next to her, chatting with some of the guests at the party. Siri said, "I am so tired—I need a nap. I'll be upstairs for a while. Will you take care of Anastasia?"

I saw Cara's face light up. She seemed honored to be the aunt chosen for this responsibility. And since she had once worked in the preemie unit of a hospital, she had a way of holding newborns to make them feel safe and secure.

It was comical to hear Cara and Maja's conversation about who got to hold the baby.

"Cara, it's my turn now. I want to hold Anastasia for a while."

"Maja, Siri gave Anastasia to me to take care of. Just a few minutes longer, and then it'll be your turn."

I heard Maja telling someone at the party, "This is a whole new adventure for me. I feel so close to Anastasia and closer to Siri too. We can both give our love to Anastasia and focus on her. I am so glad that Siri wants our help to take care of such a precious little girl."

In the first six months of Anastasia's life the aunties got many phone calls asking if they would be able to take care of her. They thoroughly enjoyed their roles as Auntie Cara and Auntie Maja.

One of my friends asked, "Now, Mary, what does it feel like to be a grandma?" I told her, "When I first saw Anastasia and Siri in the hospital, my mind flashed back to those first days with Siri. It was as if it was happening to me again." I could feel Siri's joy as no one else could. The cord of unconditional love is there from generation to generation. I could also feel the love that surrounded the family as Maja and Cara took up their roles as the aunties and the whole family offered unconditional love to its newest member.

17

A Devastating Decision and Surprising Outcome

> When we tell our stories to one another we discover that we share the same joys and tragedies, the same ambiguities and struggles.
>
> —Sue Monk Kidd

Anger, sadness, and disgust overwhelmed me. In the morning paper I'd read that the Minnesota State Legislature had passed the bill to let the people of Minnesota decide on an amendment to the state constitution stating that marriage could only be between a man and a woman. My heart sank; my hope diminished. How would the people of Minnesota react to this? I agreed with Senator John Marty (DFL, Roseville), who had introduced a bill to legalize same-sex marriage every year since 2008. He said, "No one voted on my marriage, so why should we vote on anyone else's?"

If this became law, it would be almost impossible to reverse. Republicans knew that the governor didn't have veto power over an amendment. The same people who preached about taking big government out of our lives wanted an amendment to take away others' civil rights. How could I have a calm voice about this? I went back and reviewed "The Credo of My Adversary," by Mel White. The last part of the credo says, "I believe that one day my adversary and I will understand each other and then if we conduct our search for truth guided by the principles of love, we will find a new position to satisfy us both."

Those words calmed me somewhat. But that was a big "one day," and before too long I began ranting again. Paul's constant refrain was, "I more than hear you, Mary, but why are you shouting at me?" I would reply, "It's not you I'm raging at. It's the situation. They're doing this to our daughters."

Feeling angry and so upset I could not focus on anything, frustrated to the point of throwing the dishes onto the floor instead of washing them, I found surprising words of comfort that evening while again rehearsing one of my favorite choir anthems for Sunday morning. (This song must be Spirit-led, as it seems to appear at a time when I need guidance the most.)

> Be still and know that I am God.
> I will comfort you when you come to me in your hour of
>   need.
> I will wipe your tears; you will be renewed.
> Come unto Me, My child, be still, and know that I will
>   give you rest.
> I am present in your pain and I always will remain your
>   Comforter and Friend.
> Peace I leave with you; my peace, I give unto you.
> Peace. Peace. Peace.

These words gave me some peace. But peace from God didn't mean I should do nothing. Even though my anger had been replaced with solace, I was determined to go forth in wisdom and grace with feelings of love for others. The anthem reminded me to trust and follow and know that God is with me wherever I go, and that in the end I am loved and valued, for God values everyone equally no matter what others may do. That love cannot be taken away from me. And God's love cannot be taken away from Maja and Cara either.

Angela Watrous said it so clearly in the book *50 Ways to Support Lesbian and Gay Equality*: "Opening closed minds isn't a simple task.

That's why we recommend focusing your activities less on changing people's minds and more on changing people's hearts." So I prayed for major changes in people's hearts. Acceptance was already widespread among young people. Now if we could just get them out to vote. Why must everything be a battle? *Teach me the ways of nonviolence and peace*, I prayed.

This particular group of Republican legislators felt they had the right and the power to discriminate against certain people, including my daughters. How could they be so unmoved by the stories they heard from people who would be affected by the amendment?

One day, as Cara was going out the back door, I said, "I just can't imagine how you must be feeling about the upcoming amendment vote. How dare they do such a thing?" As Cara walked down the steps to the sidewalk, she turned, looked up at me, and said, "Well, I am disappointed too, but maybe this is the beginning of a much bigger picture. I hope the amendment doesn't pass, but it may get a few more people understanding who we are. I'm willing to wait as long as I see there is some progress being made."

Cara's response caused me to again read part of Mel White's credo and repeat it several times: "I believe that my only task is to bring my adversary truth in love (nonviolence) relentlessly." It helped me every day as I went forward and told my story and Maja's.

On a Sunday not long after that, Maja and Cara were over for their usual lunch and laundry routine. We talked again about the upcoming amendment vote, and I gave them a copy of a letter Pastor Brad Froslee had posted on his Facebook page. A friend who was a member of his church had sent it to me, knowing I would be interested. Reading what he had to say helped me process some of my anger. Being a gay ELCA minister with a partner and a child as well, Pastor Froslee had the qualifications to speak in defense of voting no on this amendment. In the letter he asked important questions of the legislators: Why now? Why were they so worried about marriage? What did we really desire to see as the fabric of our society? And was it fair to use religion to demean others?

Meanwhile I read in the *New York Times* that New York had passed legislation to affirm marriage equality. What a celebration—and right before the annual Pride parade in New York City! The senate there was majority Republican too, and yet it passed. I had hoped that when the national amendment to ban same-sex marriage came up for a vote in 2012 our state would be one of the first to vote no. It would be a vote by the people, not just the legislature, and not just a verdict by the judges, as it was in Iowa.

As Maja, Cara and I were just finishing up with coffee and brownies one Sunday, Maja asked me if I wanted to go to a workshop to help people tell their stories about having LGBTQ family members—one of the ways we could change people's hearts so that the amendment would be defeated.

"I'll put it on my calendar," I said. "Cara, are you going?"

"I wish I could, but I have class that evening."

"We'll miss you."

I arrived at the workshop early, got a good seat, and saved one for Maja. Our arrival clocks differ: mine is on the early side, and hers is usually right at the appointed time. The workshop, which was sponsored by Lutherans Concerned, was in a Lutheran church in St. Paul. They expected about two hundred people.

My seat was on the aisle in the middle of the room, with a good view of those coming in and also those already there. Although I didn't recognize anyone other than the speakers, whom I knew only by their leadership roles, I still felt a sense of belonging. We were all there for the purpose of learning how to share our stories. Friends greeted each other with hugs; strangers struck up conversations. I wished Maja would arrive soon so I could give her a big hug. Being comfortable in bigger groups has always been a challenge for me, but knowing Maja would be there soon helped my anxiousness.

Maja arrived with minutes to spare. After some preliminary remarks and introductions by the organizers of the event, the training began. We learned some techniques for telling our stories effectively, and then we broke into groups of two and three to practice. Maja and I were in different groups. At first I wanted to be in a group with her, but then I realized that we shared the same story. It would be better to hear different stories and meet some new people. In the groups we asked each other questions and gave suggestions to develop our story into a short, meaningful illustration that could help someone else listen and visualize what we had to say.

At the end of the training, as Maja and I were leaving, I said, "It was interesting for me to watch you during the evening."

"Why, Mom?"

"You seemed so comfortable in this group, and I realized your maturity, too, and your willingness to share."

Maja looked at me with those hazel eyes and her half smile. She gave me a hug before we said goodbye.

All of us who'd completed the training were encouraged to sign a pledge to tell our story to at least thirty-six people in the coming months. I told my story whenever I could to whomever I encountered.

I wore my orange-and-blue "Vote No" button when I went out, and it gave me courage to step out and keep my pledge. I felt freer to tell my story. People asked me about the Vote No campaign, and I told them that I had a lesbian daughter who was married but didn't have legal rights here in Minnesota.

The 2012 Minneapolis Area Synod of the ELCA voted by a large majority to oppose the amendment and urged voters to vote no. Shortly thereafter, I had an opportunity to tell my story in a most unusual place.

The Sunday after the synod assembly I sang in our church choir for the 11:00 a.m. and noon worship services. After the first service, the choir filed downstairs to the fellowship hall for donuts and visiting time. Since I'm in the first row, I get downstairs early. I frequently stop at the bathroom. I often meet the same people in there every week, and we joke about being on the same schedule.

That Sunday morning there wasn't anyone else in the bathroom. The usual din echoed from the nursery down the hall as parents picked up their children after worship. Just outside the door is a drinking fountain where the little ones stop for some water. I came into the bathroom and took off my purple robe and the white-and-purple stole. The sleeves are long and flowing and the stole comes to a point down the back, so it is safer to take the whole thing off before going into a stall. As I was removing my robe, someone came in; I recognized her from my regular walks around Lake Harriet, where she also liked to walk.

"Hi. How are you this morning?" I asked.

"Oh, hi. I loved the anthem."

"Thanks, it's one of our favorites."

I usually pick the middle of the three stalls, and she went into the stall on my right.

"So, Mary, what did you think of the vote yesterday at the ELCA Synod Assembly?" she asked.

I replied, "I'm excited! I am so glad they voted to oppose the amendment."

There was silence for a moment, and then she said, "Really? But marriage is only between a man and a woman."

I felt my blood pressure begin to rise. I was about ready to let her have it when I remembered my training from the workshop and began to tell my story.

"We will have to disagree with each other. I have a lesbian daughter, and I am happy for her and her partner and for the support she's getting." I waited to see what she would say.

"Oh, but the Bible says . . ."

"No, the Bible doesn't mention the words *gay* and *lesbians*. I can tell you what the Bible does say if you want to talk about it sometime. And do you think Adam and Eve were married?"

The automatic flush sounded. Then there was silence as she exited her stall. As I heard the water splash and the automatic towel dispenser rolling, she made another comment that had nothing to do with our conversation. There was a pause, and it seemed to me that she might be thinking about what I had said. But all she said as she left was, "Well, have a good morning."

I don't think she went away angry. I hoped I'd have a chance to say more at some time in the future. I must have faith that, just as water dropping on a stone eventually makes a hole, such conversations will, over time, with enough effort, change hearts and minds.

The campaign was in full swing by spring of 2012. Fortunately it was also a presidential election year. That meant more people would get out and vote. No one could miss the bright orange signs with bold blue letters that read, "VOTE NO Don't Limit the Freedom to Marry." When a neighbor asked where I had gotten my sign, I offered to pick up more signs for the neighborhood.

One morning as I went through the daily routine of taking in the paper and turning off the outside light, I looked out the front window and discovered that our Vote No sign was missing. So was the sign supporting our U.S. Representative, Keith Ellison, for reelection.

"Paul, look out the window. Our signs are gone!"

"Are you sure?"

I threw up my hands and headed for the front door. Paul was right behind me. We ran outside to see if the signs had just fallen over. Our neighbors' signs were all still there, but ours were indeed gone. I hadn't heard of this happening in our neighborhood before. It puzzled me.

Later that day I replaced the signs with new ones, but this time I put them inside our front porch, taped to the window. They were not as visible, but it was a safer place to express our feelings about the upcoming vote, and they wouldn't be hidden by snow during the winter months. The other sign posted in our window also proclaimed "Vote NO 11/6/12," along with a quote: "Love does no wrong. Love fulfills the law" (Romans 13:10). When I commiserated with a friend who had also had her signs stolen, she said, "I kept replacing it with a new one. Since the signs cost ten dollars each, I finally added a note to the sign that said, 'Thanks for contributing to the Vote No campaign.'"

By early summer of 2012 Vote No signs were popping up on more and more lawns on our block and also all along Lyndale Avenue, a main route through south Minneapolis one block west of us. I saw no Vote Yes signs anywhere in our part of town.

That June, Vote No was also a big part of the theme for the Twin Cities Pride parade. On the Sunday of the festival, when the parade is held, we attended a graduation party for one of our neighbors. It's always a delight to be a part of these milestones. Many of the graduate's friends went to the parade first and then came to the open house. They arrived in orange T-shirts with "VOTE NO" in blue letters across the front. Some wore large buttons too. I noted the irony: most of these students went to South High, whose colors are orange and black. The rival high school's colors are orange and blue, but here were South students proudly wearing their rival's colors and not minding at all.

On the subject of LGBTQ civil rights, all the first-time voters seemed to be in agreement on voting no. Although I usually stay on the sidelines at parties, I found myself wanting to visit with each young person there and ask them about how they came to support the Vote No campaign. I smiled to myself, thinking, *The future generation gets it.*

During the summer months, our phone rang constantly with requests to volunteer for the Vote No campaign. Calling people to get out the vote is way out of my comfort zone, but Paul had done it for other causes and volunteered to call voters for the campaign. In the fall, on his final calling shift, he told me that the people he contacted would listen politely at first, but when he mentioned that civil rights were being taken away, they started thinking about what this vote was really all about.

One September morning another flyer appeared stuck in our front door. *Now what's this one about?* I thought. Paul appeared on the porch. I handed him the leaflet and explained, "Steve and Murray are having an informational party at their house the first week in October in support of voting no on the amendment. It'll be interesting to see who comes to support Vote No. I think most of our block is voting no. What do you think?"

"Yeah, I think so too, judging from the signs on the lawns."

At the gathering at Steve and Murray's home, there seemed to be a representative from every house on the block. Mark, who lives directly across the street from us, came to greet me and said, "I just wanted to say thanks for being the first one to put a Vote No sign on your lawn."

"Really? We were first? I didn't realize that. I hope we can defeat this amendment. It's so unfair."

I looked into Mark's face and sensed that he understood what I was saying: *I am here for you with my sign. I am willing to speak up.* I hope the warm glow I felt as he thanked me showed through with the smile on my face. I almost gave him a hug, too, but he was a new neighbor, so I stopped myself. After we had all gathered inside, Steve made a speech. Attempting unsuccessfully to hold back his tears, he thanked us all for coming. As he looked around the room filled with neighbors, he said, "When Murray and I planned this we never imagined so many people would be standing with us to vote no."

I looked around the room, observing the reaction of each neighbor, and it was difficult to keep my own tears from flowing.

That last month before the election was a constant push to get out the vote through all possible modes of communication. Paul and I attended the All Saints for All Families worship service at Hennepin Methodist Church in Minneapolis. I wished Maja and Cara could have been there to join us in experiencing that powerful evening, but by this time they had moved to Tallahassee, Florida, for Cara's internship as a Lutheran pastor.

The atmosphere of that service was Spirit led. As people gathered in the sanctuary, the volunteer team captains of Minnesotans United for All Families, the organization leading the Vote No campaign, introduced themselves and welcomed each person into the pews. Paul and I found a place to sit about three-quarters of the way toward the back. I began visiting with my neighbor, asking her questions about where she was from and why she was there. I looked around for others I knew, too, but most of them were in the processional or sitting way up in the front.

I noticed pictures on the walls of all sorts of families, from single people and their pets to same-sex couples and their children to blended families to mixed-race families. Looking at them all reminded me what *family* means. I thought that after the service I might have time to look more closely; people were crowding in, and the sanctuary was filling up.

The service began with clergy from all denominations marching down the center aisle in their robes and stoles. More than a thousand people were in attendance, and chills ran up my spine as our voices rang out together in the hymn "For All the Saints." I watched the procession of faith leaders walking together toward the front of the church, presenting a spirit of unity of purpose. I experienced that united feeling too throughout my entire body and soul.

The Twin Cities Gay Men's Chorus processed in next, wearing black T-shirts reading, "Marry Us." I wish I had remembered to wear mine, which read, "Marry Them." One of the members of the chorus told me later how overcome he was to see so many people there in support of marriage equality. The chorus lined up in front, facing the congregation. Their first song was "Walk Hand in Hand With Me." I wished they had invited the congregation to participate in it, with everyone standing and holding hands, as they do at their concerts.

Pastor Bradley Schmeling, the minister of Gloria Dei Lutheran Church in St. Paul, gave the sermon. The text for All Saints Day was John 11:32–44. It's the story about Lazarus being raised from the dead. When Pastor Bradley emphasized the words "Jesus cried in a loud voice, 'Lazarus, *come out!*'" the entire congregation applauded loudly, said, "Amen," and nodded in agreement.

The pastor also emphasized what we are to do when someone is invited to come out. The last part of the Scripture passage reads, "Jesus said to them, 'Unbind him, and let him go!'" Wow! What a message for those coming out for the first time, and also for people like me to speak up and come out as a parent and as an advocate for LGBTQ rights.

Catholics for Marriage Equality Minnesota performed the hymn "For All the Children," composed by David Lohman. They weren't allowed to record it in a Catholic church, so they had recorded it at Calvary Lutheran Church in Minneapolis. (The video on YouTube lists the forty Catholic churches represented in support of the Vote No campaign.) The song reminds me of the civil rights anthem "We Shall Overcome." Perhaps some day this hymn will be recognized in the LGBTQ rights movement as a liberation song. The congregation gathered for the All Saints service boldly sang the hymn's words of comfort and hope:

> O, may our hearts and minds be opened,
> fling the church doors open wide.
> May there be room enough for ev'ry-one inside.
> For in God there is a welcome, in God we all belong.
> May that welcome be our song.

The words leaped off the page as I joined with a thousand voices singing together. I hope that it will be included the next time the ELCA revises its hymnal.

The service ended with a candle lighting ceremony for those who had died during the past year and a prayer for the election the following Tuesday. Participating in the service gave me a sense of belonging to a larger family in which everyone was welcome and accepted for who they are. Yet I couldn't help thinking, *How would the Vote Yes people have responded if they had been here?*

Paul and I walked slowly out of the church. The people around us were also moving slowly and not talking much. Perhaps, like me, they were lost in thought about what the service meant and wondering if our prayers for equality would be answered.

The day after the service was Maja's birthday. Paul and I were in the kitchen, having breakfast. He had his usual granola and fruit, and I was fixing myself a piece of toast. Weather in Minnesota in November is usually rather gray. The leaves are gone, the grass is brown, the skies are often cloudy, and there can even be snowstorms. This particular morning it was below freezing, but our cozy kitchen with the Tiffany lamp over the table seemed cheery and bright. It was a time for a cup of tea, too. I suggested to Paul, "Let's call Maja and sing 'Happy Birthday.'" Paul ran upstairs to the office phone so we could both sing to her. It's a family tradition.

"I wish we could be with you in Tallahassee to help you celebrate," I said.

"Yeah, I'll be a bit lonely today since Cara is at a conference, but she called me earlier this morning and sang too."

"I'm glad you sent in your absentee ballots. That vote on the amendment will be a close call."

On Monday, the day before the election, my hair stylist, Joey, gave me my quarterly haircut.

At one point he said, "I know we are going to win this time."

"What makes you so sure?"

"Well, after the Hurricane Sandy storm caused all that catastrophe out East, I got this calm that came over me. It was as if our little concern here in the scheme of things is not so important. Somehow, though, I know all will be okay now."

"Yeah, but . . ."

"Mary, there are no buts this time, no buts."

"Okay, Joey, I'm with you on this one."

Minnesota voters ultimately voted no on the amendment. The vote was close: 51 percent voted to reject the amendment. For me there was relief, rejoicing, and wanting to call everyone I knew and say thank you, thank you, thank you. I wished we could have celebrated with Maja and Cara in person, but a phone call had to do for the moment.

After the election we got a postcard from Minnesotans United for All Families. I posted it on the refrigerator.

WHAT WE BUILT TOGETHER:
700 coalition partners
27,000 volunteers

67,000 donors

1.5 million voters said "NO"

The largest grassroots campaign in Minnesota history

THANK YOU

I was in joyful mode, skipping down the sidewalk of our neighborhood and still seeing many Vote No signs along the way. *Thank you, Minnesota, for doing the courageous right thing. Thanks be to God for being there through the rough times and now the joyous times too.*

There was a long road ahead, but I thought perhaps now Senator Marty could reintroduce his motion to rescind the law in Minnesota so same-sex couples could finally have the right to marry. Perhaps this time it would pass, since the legislature in Minnesota was again in the hands of the Democrats and the governor would sign the bill. And maybe Maja and Cara would be coming back to Minnesota, Cara as a Lutheran minister and Maja as a teacher. This time they could be a married couple in Minnesota.

The groups that helped to defeat the amendment were all fired up to continue—to legalize same-sex marriage. There were rallies and visits with legislators, and this time marriage equality had a real chance to become law.

I was on the outside looking in, an advocate but not directly involved. On the day of the final vote in the state house I was glued to the TV as our public television station broadcast the proceedings. There were no long delays, just speeches pro and con before the vote was taken. The observers had been instructed not to respond to the vote, so when it was announced that the bill had passed, they stayed quiet, but the people outside the chamber began to cheer. I celebrated at home by calling a few people. I wanted to share this news with the whole world, but not all would be rejoicing in the same manner or feeling the excitement I felt. I wanted to go out and dance and let my emotions take over, but with my Scandinavian reserve, that didn't happen.

The state senators would vote the following Monday. Senator Scott Dibble was front and center in the debate. In a speech he said that when the senate had voted to put a constitutional amendment to a vote, he felt defeated. But in the long run, he said, it was the best thing that happened. The people voted the amendment down, and it allowed more Democrats to be elected to state government plus a Democrat as governor.

While listening to his speech, I broke down and cried. Scott was our senator, and I had received several e-mails from him during the campaign. It amazed me that he could be so hopeful and still had faith that in the end all would turn out well. He was right; as he said, "Values that unite us are stronger than values that divide us."

All was in place. When the votes were counted, the bill passed 37 to 30, making Minnesota the twelfth state to legalize same-sex marriages. *Hallelujah! Let the rejoicing continue.*

The following Tuesday, Governor Mark Dayton signed the bill. He even moved his desk out onto the capitol steps so the crowds could witness the signing. Thousands of enthusiastic Minnesotans gathered on the lawn to witness this event.

"You changed the course of history," Governor Dayton said. "Love is now the law."

I will long remember those words. I've told many of my friends who live in other states about this amazing day. Rainbow flags flew everywhere, and one of the bridges in St. Paul was decorated end to end with large rainbow flags. (As usual, a few people called attention to all the flags. "Who paid for those?" they asked. "Was it the taxpayers in the city of St. Paul?" The answer was, "No, they were all donated. No city money was used.")

There was a march after the signing, and thousands of people walked peacefully from the state capitol through the streets of St. Paul, waving rainbow flags. Since I don't enjoy large crowds, I followed the events as they unfolded through the media. I was there in spirit while rejoicing and celebrating at home.

Another big step forward occurred at the federal level. On June 26, 2013, the Defense of Marriage Act (DOMA) was partially lifted by the Supreme Court in a five-to-four decision. Same-sex marriages were now legal as far as the federal government was concerned, but the Supreme Court decided to allow each state to rule on this decision. This meant that in thirty-seven states DOMA was still the law, but in twelve states where same-sex marriages were legal, those couples had all the same rights married couples had. Cara and Maja could now file their taxes jointly, among many other legal benefits. Yes, love was now the law in Minnesota!

On June 26, 2015, the US Supreme Court ruled that states could not deny marriage licenses to same-sex couples and must recognize same-sex couples' existing marriages. The majority concluded:

> No union is more profound than marriage, for it embodies the highest ideals of love, fidelity, devotion, sacrifice, and family. In forming a marital union, two people become something greater than once they were. As some of the petitioners in these cases demonstrate, marriage embodies a love that may endure even past death. It would misunderstand these men and women to say they disrespect the idea of marriage. Their plea is that they do respect it, respect it so deeply that they seek to find its fulfillment for themselves. Their hope is not to be condemned to live in loneliness, excluded from one of civilization's oldest institutions. They ask for equal dignity in the eyes of the law. The Constitution grants them that right.

18

Finding My Voice as an Advocate

The wise of heart is called perceptive, and pleasant speech
increases persuasiveness.

—Proverbs 16:21

Maja is lesbian, and we object to jokes about gays." That's what I
should have said. But I was caught off guard. Paul and I still
weren't sure how to tell family members about Maja. Should we make
a big announcement? Should we first put feelers out to see what their
thoughts on the subject were?

It was the summer of 2002, not long after Maja came out to us. Paul
and I were visiting my relatives in Pasadena, California. We hadn't
said anything about Maja. Everyone was at the dinner table: my second
cousins and their husbands and one of their daughters, too. (How does
that go again? Second cousin? Or is it cousin once removed?) The conversation was light; it was the kind of dinner the Danes in my family
are known for. It felt like another hyggelig, relaxing family dinner. The
good hand-painted Danish dishes were on the long Danish Modern
teak table, and the candles glowed, creating a warm atmosphere. Paul
and I sat across from each other. The hosts were seated at the end nearest the kitchen so they could serve us when we needed something.

As coffee and real Danish pastry were about to be served, someone
made a joke with a homophobic punch line. I looked at Paul, and he
looked at me. We both said nothing. We said nothing! Here was a

chance to share our story, and we said nothing. Our eyes just looked down at our food. I wanted to defend and protect my daughter, but I wasn't ready to out Maja yet. I told myself I didn't fear what they would think. Still, I just sat there and said nothing. I had not found my voice to come out myself.

When Paul and I were alone later that evening, I asked him, "So what were you thinking when he made that joke?"

"What joke?"

"You know, the one about gays?"

"Oh, that, well, I was thinking I wish I had said something to defend Maja."

"Yeah, me too. But what could we have said? Would they have listened?"

"Maybe if we had come out as parents of a lesbian, they would have accepted what we said."

I was struggling to find my voice to speak out and become an advocate. For me being an advocate would mean being in someone's corner, to cheer them on, to root for them, to pray for them too. Being an advocate for Maja would mean relentless defense, especially if she were being treated unfairly because she is lesbian. I pledged to myself that I would fight to defend and protect Maja from harm and be relentless but nonviolent in my approach.

Overprotecting Maja—not letting her fend for herself—can be harmful too. There is tension between lovingly holding her tight and lovingly letting her go in her own direction. It doesn't mean I shouldn't speak up if friends or relatives make a snide remark about being gay. It has taken some time for me to be brave enough to become an advocate and find my voice when the opportunity presents itself.

To become an effective advocate, I decided to make an effort to befriend more LGBTQ people, to learn about their experiences of discrimination and understand how they stood up for their civil rights. I wanted to act on my convictions, to speak up when I could in defense of letting everyone be who they are and not be afraid. From members of our family to my life coach to neighbors to my senator in the state legislature to writers I met taking classes at the Loft (the local literary center) to friends at church, I found wonderful people to guide me to further knowledge, understanding, and advocacy. I only had to look back to realize all these people had been gently placed in my path.

Reading books helped me become open to new experiences and new ways of telling my story to others. When I think of the first time Maja and I went to an LGBTQ bookstore together, I can't help smiling at the memory. I enjoy going to small, independent bookstores because it's so much easier to find my way around and locate the books I want to read. Amazon Bookstore in Minneapolis had the name long before the giant online company existed. It carried a wide variety of books to choose from, not just ones about sexuality.

At first Maja attempted to steer me away from some of the more suggestive sections of the store. I teased her a little: "Maja, you know I'm not into graphic books of any kind, but thanks for trying to protect me."

Maja gave me a copy of Betty DeGeneres's book *Love, Ellen: A Mother/Daughter Journey* and suggested we read it and discuss another mom and daughter's similar pilgrimage. The book is about how "love can transform ignorance to understanding and rejection to acceptance." As it has been said, with love all things are possible. Reading the book helped me see how lifting the burden of keeping something hidden inside can be such a relief. It has taken me some time to feel that freedom, to be able to talk about Maja to others.

One of our former ministers led a Bible study about acceptance. He was such a good leader that the room was filled to capacity—over a hundred people. After his presentation there were questions from the group. It didn't take long before the question about acceptance of LGBTQ people came up. I thought about saying something about our family. *Do I dare speak in front of such a large group?* I had almost worked up enough courage to contribute when Karen, who was sitting in front of me, spoke first and talked about her daughter. The pastor walked over to where she was sitting. His action told me he was empathizing and listening. The exchange between the two with the entire group listening in was definitely Spirit led. Since the subject had been brought up, I didn't add to the conversation, but I did talk to Karen after the study was over. We became friends and now support each other, knowing we walk the same path in advocating for our daughters. Because of Karen's efforts, one of our Bible study groups is for anyone who has a family member who is LGBTQ. I lovingly refer to them as the rainbow group.

One book led to another, and I found myself on a journey to dig out information on sexuality. Certain libraries in Minneapolis had better collections than others. To view the books at Luther Seminary's bookstore, I had to get out a stool because they were on the top shelf. (Perhaps that was just the way they happened to be organized, but . . .)

I knew I needed to study the Bible passages that fundamentalists like to quote when they argue that God condemns homosexuality. If you ask them to explain their view, their response is usually a vague one, starting with, "The Bible says . . ." (When Maja hears someone say this, she usually wants to reply, "But the Bible doesn't talk."). I like to ask, "Will you show me the verses you are referring to? Can we discuss them together?" The usual response: "Oh it talks about *it* being an abomination." What do they mean by *it*?

In my research I came upon Mel White's organization, Soulforce, and its website, where he discusses these verses in detail and helps explain how they can be misinterpreted. Mel White is a pastor, filmmaker, and writer. At one point he was a ghostwriter for fundamentalists such as Pat Robertson and Jerry Falwell.

I read White's books *Stranger at the Gate* and *Religion Gone Bad*. His interpretation of the Bible speaks the truth to me. His arguments have helped me when these verses come up in discussions with others. He emphasizes that the Bible is a book about God, not a book about human sexuality. That rings true, especially when I looked up how many times love is mentioned in the Bible. In the New Revised Standard Version love is mentioned over 500 times, and up until 1946 English translations of the Bible didn't even have the word "homosexuality" in it.

In Mel White's pamphlet, "What the Bible Says and Doesn't Say about Homosexuality," he constantly stresses that the Bible is a book about God and God's mighty acts out of love for us. God is the judge, not human beings. God loves us as we are, no matter what. These messages come through to me loud and clear.

The Bible passages in Genesis 19:1–14 about Sodom and Gomorrah are often misinterpreted. God destroyed the cities because its people didn't take God seriously about caring for the poor, the hungry, the outcast, and the homeless.

Leviticus 18:22 and 20:13 describe two males having sex as an abomination. In those days the understanding was that the man's sperm contained the whole child. The woman's womb just provided the incubating space. So two men spilling semen without the possibility of producing a child was considered murder. The abomination was murder, not the sexual act.

When I have shared this interpretation with others, they seem somewhat surprised. It makes sense to me: they're experiencing a kind of enlightenment. Several friends have asked for a copy of White's interpretations so they too can read another point of view and be more informed on the subject. This is why being well informed is such a big part of my advocacy. I have a tendency to be judgmental when family members express opinions and I know they haven't read anything on the subject.

As my emotions directed me toward acting on what I had learned, I struggled with how to respond. Sometimes I felt the urge to hit someone over the head to get their undivided attention! But I realized this was not the way to persuade anyone. I came across a line from Proverbs that I posted on my refrigerator: "The wise of heart is called perceptive, and pleasant speech increases persuasiveness" (Proverbs 16:21).

The nonviolent philosophies of Gandhi, Dr. Martin Luther King Jr., and Mel White became my guide. "Attack the false idea, not the person who holds that idea," King insisted. He strove to put into practice Jesus's command to "love your enemies," even while sitting in a jail cell, being taunted by those enemies. "We can only persuade our adversaries on the basis of truth alone," he said, "not by resorting to half-truth, exaggeration, or lie." Every volunteer in King's organization pledged to follow eight principles, including "meditate daily on the teachings and life of Jesus, walk and talk in the manner of love, and observe with both friend and foe the ordinary rules of courtesy." Wow! If only we all pledged to live by those values. If only I could live by those values.

The command to attack the idea and not the person is such a challenge for me. When someone makes negative statements about my daughters, I react instinctively, without thinking. To attack the idea gently can be so difficult, and yet it has been proven in the long run to be the better way. A civil discourse can provide food for thought and perhaps a change of heart.

Reflecting back on my college years in the mid-1960s, I remembered that even then I had been working on being an advocate for justice. One of my daily rituals during my college years was to go to the library and read the paper. I wanted to know what was happening in the real world, especially with the civil rights movement. President Johnson had just signed the Civil Rights Act into law. On the morning I saw the pictures of Addie Mae Collins, Cynthia Wesley, Carole Robertson, and Denise McNair, four black children who had been killed in the bombing of the Sixteenth Street Baptist Church in Birmingham, Alabama, I knew I needed to step up and support the families grieving for their children.

That morning in chapel, Pastor Pete spoke about the tragedy and urged students to organize a march in honor of the children, to let people know how much we cared. Empathy and concern permeated the entire congregation. Hearts were ripped open. Tears flowed. I knew then that I needed to join and march for justice and solidarity.

About three hundred students—one-fifth of the total student body—gathered in the gym that also served as the chapel in those days. The march was the number-one subject on campus that week. Some students were apprehensive, but many of my friends committed to supporting Dr. King's nonviolent movement. Taking a stand and defending people's civil rights was certainly an idea that I, as a Lutheran, could support. Martin Luther took a stand way back in the 1500s, and Martin Luther King Jr. was also taking a stand.

As we prepared to march, Pastor Pete, with his clear bass voice, warned us that there might be some opposition. We were to march in silence from campus to the middle of town. Before leaving, we bowed our heads and Pastor Pete led us in prayer for the families grieving in Alabama. We sang the hymn "In Christ There Is No East or West." The volume of voices ringing out stirred empathy in me. As I marched, I thought of how the families must be grieving for their children. I prayed that God would be with the entire group of marchers as we walked in support of nonviolent paths to peace and justice.

I could hear the shuffle of feet as we moved along, and I focused on looking straight ahead. I sensed that the tragedy was enlarging the circle of grief, making it bigger and bigger until it slowly encompassed the entire country. Even way up north in Sioux Falls, South Dakota, students were marching in support of the civil rights movement. I was learning to speak out with my feet in defense of injustice done to the black community.

I can't say there was peace in my heart as I walked, and forgiveness wasn't there either, but a spark of hope emerged that maybe someone watching would be moved to join in the movement for justice. I was beginning to realize that one person could make a difference.

In the spring of 2005 I went to the Minnesota state capitol to meet with legislators and participate in a rally in support of LGBTQ rights. My former pastor, Lowell Erdahl, was one of the speakers at the rally, and I drove there with my life coach and her partner. We also met a group from St. Paul-Reformation Lutheran Church. One of them thanked me and said, "We [LGBT people] are only about ten percent of the population, so we need straight people to come and help."

If I could now come to a rally at the state capitol to right a wrong done to someone else, wasn't that also what Jesus's teachings were all about? Love one another, and serve one another too.

As I was formulating my ideas about being a nonviolent advocate, one of my writing teachers pointed out that violence had also been part of the LGBTQ rights movement. At that point I began to read more about the history of the movement. I learned about the Stonewall riots in New York City.

"Early on the morning of Saturday, 28 June 1969, lesbian, gay, bisexual, transgender and questioning persons rioted following a police raid on the Stonewall Inn, a gay bar at 43 Christopher Street, New York City," writes David Carter in *Stonewall: The Riots That Sparked the Gay Revolution.* By 1969 LGBTQ people in New York City had reached the boiling point in dealing with persecution from the police. As Carter explains, "This riot and further protests and rioting over the following nights were the watershed moment in the modern LGBTQ rights movement and the impetus for organizing LGBTQ pride marches on a much larger public scale."

At our church I facilitated a Bible study. We were discussing a passage in Philippians about including everyone, and the subject of LGBTQ people came up. At that point I was ready to defend them with a "relentless nonviolent" approach. But then one of the more conservative members of our group spoke up, saying, "We all know that gays are born that way." Everyone in the group nodded in approval of his statement, and we moved on to another point in the text. It took me by complete surprise that they all recognized being gay as not a choice, but a way of being. I had been ready to use my voice to advocate, but this time it wasn't necessary.

At a particularly low point in Maja and Cara's life, Cara was waiting for a call to ministry in the ELCA and was losing hope. I wanted to do something to cheer them up. Then I got a letter from Reconciling-Works: Lutherans for Full Participation, which was asking for donations to further its work as advocates for Lutheran LGBTQ pastors having difficulty finding their place in the church and getting that first call. They also asked for people to share their stories online. So I submitted one, not knowing if they would use it.

A little while later, Maja called and told me she'd seen my story on the ReconcilingWorks Facebook page. When I checked the page, I saw the picture of Maja and Cara coming down the aisle after their union ceremony, along with the story I'd written.

> I am a mom of a lesbian daughter, Maja Knutson. She has a partner/wife, Cara Knutson. Cara took our last name when they were married in Iowa in 2009.
>
> I am here for them and have been their advocate.
>
> Cara is up for call in the ELCA Region 3 where she was placed, but she received the sad news that there were no openings for her. She was then referred back to her home synod, which is St. Paul, MN. We are all feeling Maja and Cara's rejection and wondering what will happen next.
>
> Will there be a place for Cara as a pastor in the Lutheran church? Cara has been interning as a chaplain at Gundersen Lutheran Hospital in La Crosse, Wisconsin, this year, but as of August that internship is finished and then what?
>
> Paul and I have supported ReconcilingWorks through the years and know this situation is not new. . . . I also know we need to tell our stories to as many people as we can and I have been doing that and I am even writing a book entitled *Maja and Me*, the story of a mom and her lesbian daughter.
>
> I pray that there will be a place for Cara and Maja as they feel their call. We are clinging to this verse from Romans 12:12: *Rejoice in hope, be patient in suffering, persevere in prayer.*

Though I normally have nothing to do with Facebook, I'd felt our family's story was important enough to tell a wide audience. Maja and Cara said my letter to ReconcilingWorks truly brightened their day. They were proud of me for speaking out in such a broad public forum.

In 2013 I attended another weeklong writing workshop at the Madeline Island School of the Arts. For four summers I had sat next to another workshop participant named Shelley. We hadn't talked much during the week; we were both concentrating on our writing. But that day, Shelley turned to me, gave me a big hug, and said, "Mary, you are the best mom and advocate for gay rights that I know. Thank you."

19

Discovering, Changing, and Letting Go

It was time for mother-daughter to let go. It was time for us
to grow.

—Betty DeGeneres, from her memoir, *Love, Ellen*

On August 1, 2013, the day Minnesota celebrated the first time
same-sex couples could legally be married in our state, Maja and
Cara returned from their year in Florida. I felt that was a symbolic day
of acceptance and joy. Minnesota was welcoming them back with open
arms.

I had finally come to grips with some of my personal flaws. I now
acknowledged how controlling I could be. I mean well, of course! I
only wanted to help and make the situation better. This dawned on me
when I discovered that my body was out of alignment and decided to
seek help from a chiropractor. As I learned how to do certain exercises,
I noticed how difficult it was for me to relax my neck muscles. Everything else would crack and be revitalized, but the muscles in my neck
were stiff.

Dr. Matt, my chiropractor, would say, "Now Mary, just relax that
neck. Breathe in; breathe out. And relax. Come on, Mary, relax." I
would try to relax, but my neck wouldn't respond. I began calling myself "stiff-necked."

I recalled the phrase "stiff-necked people" from the Old Testament.
Moses accused the Israelites of being stiff-necked people, and God told

Moses to forgive them. For me being stiff-necked meant wanting to be in control. I have a plan, and my plan is better than your plan. Wouldn't it be better to follow what I have suggested? I've often felt frustrated when my family doesn't follow my suggestions. Now I asked myself, *Why do I feel the need to be in control?*

This whole idea finally penetrated my consciouness when I was talking with Maja on the phone. She and Cara were about to move back to La Crosse after their year in Tallahassee. Most of their belongings were in a storage unit in Minneapolis; some were stored at our house. I was in the midst of trying to organize the move for them. I heard Cara in the background: she was giving Maja her suggestions. Meanwhile, I was giving Maja my suggestions. Then there was an uncomfortable silence. I began to see that Maja was caught in the middle. I wanted her to hear my practical ideas, but I realized I needed to back off. To my way of thinking I'm the practical one in the family; I can see a simpler way to solve a problem. Now a little voice in the back of my head was saying, "Mary, you are doing it again—being controlling."

I had to face the fact that I wasn't in Maja and Cara's canoe. I wasn't in charge of steering or even paddling it at all. With that realization, I experienced an unexpected release of tension. (Perhaps my stiff neck would now relax for Dr. Matt.). I'd be happy to hear about their adventures, but I wouldn't be orchestrating their lives. *Well, maybe one more time?*

Maja and Cara couldn't come to La Crosse to look for an apartment before they moved. Cara looked at rentals online, but it would be better to have someone check the places out in person. Paul and I offered to drive to La Crosse and look at apartments for them. It's a three-hour drive, so we decided to make a day of it.

Maja and Cara seemed most appreciative of the plan. Cara found five possible apartments online. She told us that she would call and let the managers know when we'd be there.

Because we aren't tech savvy, Paul and I didn't connect with those who were to show us the apartments. Paul had studied the manual for his new cell phone but couldn't figure out how to retrieve messages. My lack of tech skills didn't help. He finally gave up, and we just enjoyed the day, explored La Crosse as we looked for the possible apartments, and stopped for a leisurely dinner on the way home. Meanwhile, Cara and Maja got a phone call from the agent we were supposed to contact in La Crosse when we didn't show up. Maja called our neighbors and my sister and brother-in-law to ask if they knew where we were. Maja and Cara were worried that we had been in an accident.

When we arrived home, our answering machine had recorded several messages of concern. When I talked to Maja, she let me know how worried she was, but she also admitted that she now understood how I worried about her.

I tried not to ask lots of questions about Maja and Cara's plans. They seemed to get overwhelmed when I did that. I was finally taking a page out of my mom's book. When she was still alive, she lived in California, and I was in Minnesota. When I called her—and that wasn't too often—she would answer the phone in her wonderful Danish accent and say, "Is that you, Mary?"

We would have a delightful conversation, and she was such a good listener. Now I am assuming her role as the matriarch. Mom was always glad to hear from me but didn't ask all kinds of questions about what was going on in our lives. Many times she would tell us she was happy that we had called: "I don't have to worry about you any more. You seem settled and happy with a family of your own to take care of."

Would I be able to continue doing this? I hoped so, but perhaps it would have to be with reminders from Maja and Cara. Perhaps we could work out a signal if I began trying to manage their lives. They could gently say "La la light bulb" or another silly saying from *Sesame Street* to alert me to what I was doing.

Once again Paul and I flitted from window to window every time we heard a car drive past. Maja and Cara had stopped in La Crosse first to see their apartment, drop off some of their things, and leave their three cats there. (I'm allergic to cats, and my daughters know that although

I like cats, they are not welcome in our house.) Finally they arrived, and we ran out to their car to meet them. I gave them each a big hug. I was excited to welcome them back. We had a party for them, and I had fixed curried chicken for dinner, with almond cake for dessert. Their friend Paul had driven up from Sioux Falls for a few days to help them pack for the move to La Crosse.

True to my word, I had not asked for any details about the move. As we were chatting, Maja casually mentioned, "I hope it's okay if we stay here for a few days."

With a slight hesitation I replied, "Oh, sure, but I thought you were going to pick up the truck tomorrow and move everything to the apartment right away."

"Well, we decided we needed a few days to just relax. Oh yeah, we also found out if we rent the truck on Sunday instead of before the weekend starts, we'll save three hundred dollars."

So they wanted to come home and use our house for R & R. It was another "surrender to surprise" for me. Surrendering for me this time became a challenge. I needed to be empathetic to this transition for them. Cara had been crying off and on all the way from Tallahassee. They already missed all the good friends they had made during Cara's internship. But they were happy to finally be in Minnesota after two grueling days of travel with three cats in a packed van.

I'm not used to having lots of people in the house anymore, and going from two people to five people for five days was a bit overwhelming. With one bathroom, I was up at 6:00 a.m. so others could take their turns later.

I had prepared some food in advance, so it was a self-serve kitchen for breakfast and lunch. The smell of coffee greeted everyone each morning, but they were on their own for breakfast. I tried to go about my own business, but I wasn't used to everyone being on his or her own schedule. I also knew that I was very protective of our home. I would say, "Come on in and make yourself at home," but that didn't mean that guests, including family members, shouldn't respect the rules of the house: take your shoes off at the door, rinse your dishes and put then in the dishwasher, hang wet towels on the assigned bathroom towel rack, push the shower curtain back so the steam can come out into the room and not cause mold, turn off lights and fans if you leave a room. These are just simple little things that make me happy.

One thing I know about myself: I need alone time. I found myself going into the bedroom, shutting the door, and attempting to do some writing. I know I could not have survived having a large family.

Still, things were going along fairly well. I knew they didn't have much money. Cara had finished her internship, and Maja's job had ended, so it was only a matter of time before the money issue came up.

On Saturday Maja finally asked me, "Could we borrow some money to pay for the truck rental?" I looked at her and without a word went to the desk for my checkbook. I wrote out a check, and they went off to the bank to deposit it. They decided to take out cash to pay for the rental truck. I didn't know all the details, nor did I want to know.

On Sunday they picked up the truck, drove to their storage unit and loaded up their belongings, drove to La Crosse, unloaded the truck, and drove back to Minneapolis.

On Monday morning I came downstairs early and encountered their friend Paul in the kitchen. He was in a panic because he had realized that the monthly payments taken directly out of his bank account were due that day. He had used his credit card to help with expenses for Maja and Cara too, and now he didn't have enough in his account to cover the bills. Lots of discussion went on between him, Maja, and Cara. I tried to stay in the background, but that became difficult.

By that time I had just about had it with everyone. It seemed people were everywhere, and there was no place for me to escape. I went into the bathroom and straightened up, pushing back the shower curtain again, setting all the shampoo bottles back in their places. I was working myself up into a state of frustration, muttering under my breath about being the mother to all these children in my home. Then, as I was leaving the bathroom, I almost ran into Cara in the hallway. She was carrying her wet towel. The day before someone had hung a soggy towel on a wooden chair in the bedroom. It was the chair I had just gotten refinished, too.

I snapped and said, "Cara, I hope you aren't going to put that towel on the chair in your bedroom." She just stood there and didn't say anything. I took the towel, and she walked into the bedroom and closed the door. I was surprised that she didn't object or try to explain.

Later she came into our bedroom where I was sitting at my desk and tried to let me know that I had hurt her feelings. I told her that I could only hold things in so long. She just happened to be there when I let it out.

Later I decided to go out on the front porch to look out into the flower garden and let nature and the singing birds soothe my temper. Maja came out and flung herself into the chair across from me. She looked at me and said, "You owe Cara an apology."

My immediate reaction was to stomp back into the house, but then I thought, *No, I'd better stay and resolve this situation.* Still, I was hurt by Maja's demand. I slumped down in my chair, and a stony silence enveloped us. As I began to calm down, I thought, *I guess this is as it should be—Maja coming to Cara's defense.* I had also realized that it was a blue towel that had been hung on the chair, and Cara usually had a green one. So she wasn't at fault, and I should have realized that.

I still didn't think I needed to apologize. It's our home, and they could respect that or leave. Maja and I started hurling accusations at each other. Maja yelled, "When are you going to quit being so controlling and let me run my own life?"

I tried to stay calm as I said, "Yes, you want to be independent. I want you to be independent. I know I'm controlling, and I'm trying not to be. What am I supposed to do when things aren't going well for you and there's no money because there is no job to rely on? What can be done to make this situation better?"

I resented being accused of being controlling of her life. I had been trying so hard not to do that. I knew I had overreacted. There was another uncomfortable silence. I was hurting, on the verge of tears, but deep down I knew Maja was right. I needed to take the advice of one of my friends who has learned what works when these situations arise with our adult children. We will listen to their concerns but remind ourselves, *This is their life, and they will figure it out.*

As Maja and I both simmered down and began speaking in moderate tones, we agreed we needed to be more truthful with each other. Cara was subdued the rest of the day, even after we had a conversation to clear the air. She was looking at her computer and not interested in talking to me. I worried that I had lost her respect—and Maja's too.

The next day they were going to drive back to La Crosse, but I had to leave the house before they were up. I knocked on their door to say goodbye, but there was no answer. So I left after writing a short note wishing them good luck. I also packed up some starter groceries, such as Cheerios and homemade granola. I set the bag by the door and left.

When I came back from quilting, they were gone. Maja had left a little note attached to the coffee pot that said, "You make the best coffee."

I often wonder, *Why can't things work out better for Maja?*

Maja soon got a couple of part-time jobs, and I was relieved. But I still had concerns. Had Maja attempted to do too much? They had no built-in support group this time. Maja and Cara had each other, but their schedules didn't give them much time together. I was trying to find a balance between my love and my instinct to control things. Perhaps we had gotten off the merry-go-round and gotten on the teeter-totter. It takes so much practice to get that balance just right. Now it was up to Cara and Maja to balance their lives. I'd stay on the sidelines but offer them my encouragement and spiritual support.

20

Suspended in a Blizzard Again

Be strong and courageous. Do not be frightened or discouraged, for the Lord your God is with you wherever you go.

—Joshua 1:9

It was officially spring, 1997, but we could see foreboding dark clouds overhead. Snow began swirling, and the wind increased till it reached gale strength. Visibility was down to one car length, and the windshield wipers were icing up.

Paul, Maja, and I were on our way to Sioux Falls via always-windy and stormy Interstate 90. Maja wanted to visit Augustana one more time before she made the big decision of where she wanted to go to college.

Now, in the middle of a blizzard, it felt as if we were suspended in air. The snow came at us sideways, and the wind blew so hard that it was difficult to keep the car going straight down the road. Paul was driving, and Maja and I had our eyes glued to the windows, looking for a rest stop or town where we could get out of this tense, panicky situation.

That moment of floating in air, not knowing where we were headed, has been imprinted in my mind. Although it happened many years ago, I can still put myself in that blizzard and be scared all over again, not knowing if we would survive.

More than fifteen years later we were back in that same suspended state, not knowing which direction we would go or if there would be a clear path to take. This time, Cara was with us. She had completed all work necessary for the call to ministry in the ELCA. She got word that she would be placed in Region 3: North Dakota, South Dakota, and greater Minnesota. (The ELCA divides the United States into nine regions, and each region is divided into synods.) She told me that the next step was for the six synod bishops in that region to meet and see where the openings for pastors might be. I wasn't too happy to hear about the region. Would there be a place for a lesbian pastor there? It sounded like blizzard conditions again. I just said I would be praying for her.

After another two weeks of waiting, I got a call from Cara and Maja. The news was devastating. The bishops told her there were no openings for her.

I was disappointed and angry at the way the whole thing was handled. Cara was willing to go anywhere in the country but was told to write down her preferences. If the ELCA knew there would be no openings in the region for Cara, why did they assign her to it? Women generally had to wait longer before getting a call, and because of the economy many ministers who would have retired were staying on in their parishes. After five years of working toward this goal, now what?

I found a verse in the chapter assigned for Bible study that week: "Rejoice in hope, be patient in suffering, persevere in prayer" (Romans 12:12). Our family had rejoiced in hope. We had to somehow keep persevering with our prayers and attempt to be patient in suffering. *How long, Lord? How long?* Waiting for a call into ministry in the Lutheran church could take months or even years. Cara was assigned to the St. Paul Synod but still lived in La Crosse, Wisconsin. She wasn't close to a supportive community in which she could talk about her situation. I think this was an all-time low for my daughters. They didn't call or e-mail. It was as if they had withdrawn into a depressed state of "Now what?"

Finally Cara sent me her thoughts.

> I love the Lutheran church, Lutheran theology, the way
> we worship, and the way we reach out to our neighbors,

and I very much would love to find a little church some-
where, like Peace Lutheran Church or St. Stephen, that
would welcome Maja and me in as their pastor. But is
that possible? I don't seem to be seeing that right now.

For so long my being gay didn't seem like this insur-
mountable obstacle. I knew my parents weren't going to
support me, but I knew that they don't support me in lots
of ways. But I was able to meet Maja, get married, and
live a fairly normal life without really any major problems. Now my being gay has become this hurtful thing
that not only hurts others but hurts me too. This is all
very new for me. Sometimes I feel so sad and lost it physically hurts, other times I feel excited about possibilities
that haven't been uncovered yet.

And what about Maja and her future? She was slowly completing
classes for her master's degree in ESL so she could teach English to
adults. She continued to work at Head Start, providing love and gentleness in teaching the very young about discovering new ideas and
getting along with each other.

Perhaps I hadn't described the situation well enough for people to
truly comprehend what a sad time this was for Maja and Cara. Our
friends hadn't walked in their shoes. When I told friends and relatives
what was happening, I didn't hear the empathy I expected. I felt lost
not knowing whom to call for support. I knew that with God's help we
would weather this blizzard, but I really wanted to cry on someone's
shoulder.

Maja and Cara had gotten snippets of information and tips on work,
but finding jobs that would pay the bills and create stability was going
to be a challenge. They were starting all over again in a new place. Were
we all heading back to that financial support merry-go-round again?
In other professions, especially the arts, a benefactor often comes to
the rescue. Why couldn't the ELCA visualize what it must be like for

pastors up for call with nothing available for them because of who they are?

So we all waited again for the blizzard to subside, the path to clear, and the skies to turn blue. I was in prayer mode, support mode, comfort mode for my daughters, wanting to help them but knowing all I could provide was supportive listening and words of hope.

I was reminded of the verse that Siri had shared with me years ago when she was driving off to Chicago despite predicted bad weather: "Be strong and courageous. Do not be frightened or discouraged, for the Lord your God is with you wherever you go" (Joshua 1:9).

Epilogue

Life must be understood backward but must be lived forward.
—Søren Kierkegaard

Once again I found myself flitting from window to window. I looked outside whenever I heard a car drive by, hoping that Maja had finally arrived. She was driving up from Storm Lake, Iowa. Fortunately it was May and no snowstorms or tornados were predicted.

Another car slowed down, and I peered out the window again. Yes, it was turning into our driveway. Paul had heard it too, and we both casually made our way to the back door so we could greet Maja. It always seems to take Maja a long time to get out of the car. I straightened up the newspapers on the kitchen table for the umpteenth time in anticipation of her arrival. It was all I could do to prevent myself from running out the back door and throwing my arms open wide to greet her with a great big hug. Finally the door opened, and Maja walked in.

Maja had come home to attend a concert by the Cavani String Quartet. Her cousin Kirsten was the violist in the group, and Maja wanted to hear them once more before Kirsten moved on to a new position, teaching viola at Oberlin College. Cara was now a chaplain at Methodist Manor in Storm Lake, Iowa. Cara generously stayed home this time to take care of their little foster child. The rules say the child cannot leave the state. I missed Cara but was glad to have time with Maja before she headed back to Iowa.

Whenever Maja comes home, I fix curried chicken for supper. We had just enough time to share her favorite dish before we headed off to the concert.

A reception followed the concert in celebration of my sister and brother-in-law's fiftieth wedding anniversary. There were so many people there to greet from years past, and I took great joy in seeing Maja conversing with the quartet members, especially her cousin and other friends she knew from years ago.

Maja has a gentle way of visiting with others, looking at each person and listening to what they have to say. I observed this from a distance, wishing that I could be in on those conversations. When Maja talked with her four-year-old niece, Anastasia, she bent down and gave her full attention, as if Anastasia was the only one in the room.

I couldn't help but reflect on how far we had come and how far I have progressed in not attempting to orchestrate Maja's life. I do wish she would call more often, just to check in. Oops! Sometimes I revert, but not as frequently now. It's the new me. When Maja does tell me about a dilemma, I still want to fix it for her, but I'm able to step back and say to myself, *Not my problem, not my concern. I'm here to listen and perhaps make a suggestion or two.* Oh yes, I still worry and run through all the possible scenarios, but I try to point my mind in a different direction. I might send a day-brightening card or e-mail some positive thoughts.

Maja was heading back to Storm Lake the next morning, but there was still time for one cup of tea and a short visit in the living room on the love seat. We chatted about the evening's events, but I reflected on times gone by. So many important conversations had happened right there in our hyggelig living room, sitting together on this love seat. We'd shared tensions, sadness, and frustrations, but also happiness, excitement, and joy. I was so thankful to God for guiding Maja and me through our times of darkness. I had faith that I would not be afraid; I'd look upward and travel onward. And I'd encourage Maja to continue looking upward and traveling onward into a future of hope.

Postlude

Sun skips across water
Squinting through eyelashes
Sparklers skimming to me

—Mary Rose Knutson

In the bow of the canoe I grasp the top of the paddle with my right hand, pushing downward. My other hand, halfway down the paddle, relaxing around the wood, gently pulls and sends us gliding forward through the clear azure water. Maja rudders her paddle expertly and sends us in a new direction. Silence reigns except for the drip, drip of the water and the shushing sound when the paddles enter for another simultaneous stroke. The smells of musty lifejackets and suntan lotion permeate the air. Maja steers us over near the rocky shoreline.

"Look out for that boulder," I tell her. "Slow us down!" Then: "Quit that!" My hand flies to my neck. I feel something cold running down my back. I turn to see Maja's Cheshire-cat grin and her paddle over my head, letting the water drip on me.

That moment of understanding flashes between us, and we break into laughter and song:

> My paddle's keen and bright
> Flashing with silver
> Follow the wild goose flight
> Dip, dip and swing.

The song drifts off. Our breathing is deep, almost in sync with the rhythm of our arms moving forward and back, forward and back. We paddle in silence—sometimes stopping to just gaze, sometimes holding our paddles up so the water drips into the lake.

My thoughts drift back to Bishop Krister Stendahl's observation: "water dripping on a stone—it makes a hole/whole not by its weight but by constantly dropping." The message for me is clearer now. It's gone from the muddy Mississippi River to sparkling-clear Lake Superior. I'm to love Maja, but this kind of love must be patient, kind, and gentle. I have become the listener, only giving advice when asked.

Maja's now in the stern of the canoe, picking the pathway, steering in a direction of her own choosing. I'm still attempting to give advice, but I'm not in control. I have become one of those drops of water gently helping others along as we paddle together, balancing our canoe. I'm the advocate for this orchestrated reality. Out of rejection, shunning, and banishment evolve dignity, grace, and freedom.

For Further Reading

Carter, David. *Stonewall: The Riots That Sparked the Gay Revolution.* New York: St. Martin's Press, 2004.

Clausen, Lars. *Straight Into Gay America: My Unicycle Journey for Equal Rights.* Washington, DC: Soulscapers, 2006.

DeGeneres, Betty. *Love, Ellen: A Mother/Daughter Journey.* New York: HarperCollins, 1999.

LaSala, Michael C. *Coming Out, Coming Home: Helping Families Adjust to a Gay or Lesbian Child.* New York: Columbia University Press, 2010.

Maran, Meredith, and Angela Watrous, editors. *50 Ways to Support Lesbian and Gay Equality: The Complete Guide to Supporting Family, Friends, Neighbors—or Yourself.* San Francisco: Inner Ocean Publishers, 2005.

McDougall, Bryce, editor. *My Child Is Gay: How Parents React When They Hear the News.* Canberra, Australia: Southwood Press, 2006.

White, Mel. "What the Bible Says—and Doesn't Say—about Homosexuality." Soulforce. http://www.psa91.com/pdf/whatthebiblesays. Accessed February 13, 2018.

Credits

Bible Quotations

Unless otherwise indicated, biblical passages are from the New Revised Standard Version, copyright 1989, Division of Christian Education of the National Council of the Churches of Christ in the United States of America. Used by permission. All rights reserved.

Biblical passages marked ESV are taken from THE HOLY BIBLE, ENGLISH STANDARD VERSION®, copyright © 2001 by Crossway, a publishing ministry of Good News Publishers. Used by permission.

The biblical passage marked NASU is taken from the NEW AMERICAN STANDARD UPDATED BIBLE®, copyright © 1995 by The Lockman Foundation. Used by permission.

The biblical passage marked NIV is from THE HOLY BIBLE, NEW INTERNATIONAL VERSION® NIV®, copyright © 1973, 1978, 1984, 2011 by Biblica, Inc.® Used by permission. All rights reserved worldwide.

The biblical passage marked NKJV is from the New King James Version, copyright © 1982 by Thomas Nelson, Inc. Used by permission. All rights reserved.

The biblical passage marked TPT is from the Passion Translation®, copyright © 2017 by BroadStreet Publishing® Group, LLC. Used by permission. All rights reserved.

Song Lyrics

Pages ix–x: Lyrics from "Here I Am, Lord," by Daniel L. Schutte (music and text) © 1981 OCP, 5536 NE Hassalo, Portland, OR 97213. All rights reserved. Used with permission.

Pages 70–71: Lyrics from "Come Unto Me and Wait," by Mark Hayes (music) and Herb Frombach (lyrics), based on Isaiah 46:31 and Psalm 46:10 © 2006 by Beckenhorst Press, Inc., Columbus, Ohio. All rights reserved. Used with permission.

Page 89: Lyrics from "Be Still," by Mary McDonald (music) and Herb Frombach (lyrics), based on Psalm 46:10 © 2010 Beckenhorst Press, Inc., Columbus, Ohio. All rights reserved. Used with permission.

Page 98: Lyrics from "For All the Children," by David Lohman (music and text) © David Lohman Music. Used by permission.

Questions for Reflection and Discussion

1. What would your response be if a family member came out to you? Do you think it might be different now that you've read Mary and Maja's story?

2. In your family, are you the oldest of the siblings, a middle child, the youngest, or an only child? How does birth order help or hinder your understanding of sibling situations?

3. Has there been a time in your life when someone you met seemed to have been placed in your path for a reason? What did you learn from that experience?

4. What kinds of resources help you learn about something new? Do you prefer to read information (in books, online, and so forth) and try to absorb it on your own? Or do you seek out experts you can talk to or learn from?

5. Do you think minds can be changed from rejection to acceptance? What can make that change happen?

6. When a person experiences many disappointments and rejections, they'll often lose self-confidence and doubt their abilities. How do you think a parent or other close loved one can help this situation in a supportive (and not enabling) way?

7. If you're a parent, when you imagine your child bringing their new significant other home to meet you, how would you make them feel welcome? Would it be different if their partner were the same gender?

8. Reinhold Niebuhr wrote, "Nothing we do, however virtuous, can be accomplished alone; therefore, we are saved by love. No virtuous act is quite as virtuous from the standpoint of our friend or foe as it is from our own standpoint. Therefore we must be saved by the final form of love, which is forgiveness." What is your own experience with the "final form of love"? Have you struggled to forgive someone?

9. What are examples of some of the blizzards in your life? What caused them? What helped you navigate safely through them?

10. What does it mean to you to be an advocate? If you feel strongly about an ideal or a principle, how do you express that feeling? Is there anything you'd be willing to risk your reputation, your friendships, or your family relationships to fight for?

Acknowledgments

In Danish I would say, *mange, mange tak*, many, many thanks to the following people for their encouragement and guidance in allowing this book to come out into the world.

To Mary Carroll Moore for all the classes at the Loft and the six workshops at Madeline Island that helped me learn the process of creating a book.

To Beth Wright for guiding me into that process of my point of view and helping me bring out my emotions. For sharing her knowledge of the publishing world. I am forever grateful.

To Ashley Finch for the creative cover design, Kellie Hultgren for copyediting, Peter Stratmoen, photography, and Zan Ceeley, proofreader and logo designer.

To the Loft Literary Center in Minneapolis for providing a variety of classes to assist writers in their craft and encouraging their creative spirit.

To Madeline Island School of the Arts (MISA) in La Pointe, Wisconsin, a place apart providing workshops for writers.

Mange tak to my writing companions Kathy Pollock, Anita Makar, and Judith Mattison, who have been my inspiration and lifeline through the past eight years.

To Pastor Lowell Erdahl, Pastor Gretchen Enoch, Joyce Pedersen, and Marilyn Sharpe, my spiritual supporters.

To Charles Yancey, Janet Greenlees, Jerry O'Neill, Marilyn Sharpe, Dori Belden, and Talia Ortiz for being my beta readers, giving me their heartfelt encouragement for the book.

To Lowell Erdahl, Anita Hill, Jerry O'Neill, Marilyn Sharpe, and Carol Throntveit for writing endorsements.

To Hollis Fricek and Joey Nytes for their support and suggestions along the way and to Dr. Matt Amundgaard, my chiropractor, who helped me to become less stiff-necked.

To my family and friends who have encouraged and supported Maja and me every step of the way: many, many thanks.

And finally, thanks be to God for that persistent tap on the shoulder and for guiding our family through the rough and smooth waters on life's journey.

CPSIA information can be obtained
at www.ICGtesting.com
Printed in the USA
BVHW08s0327020618
517880BV00007B/114/P